T0303057

Return to Naples

Return to Naples

My Italian Bar Mitzvah and Other Discoveries

ROBERT ZWEIG

FORT LEE, NEW JERSEY

Published by Barricade Books Inc.
185 Bridge Plaza North
Suite 308-A
Fort Lee, NJ 07024

www.barricadebooks.com

Library of Congress Cataloging-in-Publication Data
    Zweig, Robert, 1955-
    Return to Naples : my italian bar mitzvah and other discoveries / Robert
Zweig. p. cm.
    Includes bibliographical references and index.
    ISBN 978-1-56980-351-6 (hard cover : alk. paper)
    1. Zweig, Robert--Childhood and youth. 2. Jews--New York (State)--New
York--Biography. 3. Zweig, Robert--Travel--Italy--Naples. 4. Naples (Italy)--
Description and travel. 5. New York (N.Y.)--Biography. I. Title.

    F128.9.J5Z94 2008
    914.5'7310492092--dc22
    [B]
                                        2008020743

ISBN 13: 978-1-56980-351-6
ISBN 1-56980-351-X

                    10 9 8 7 6 5 4 3 2 1

            Manufactured in the United States of America

Contents

—𝔪—

Chapter One

—⚬—

Walking with Nonno

I ran down the gangplank of the SS *Vulcania* after a transatlantic sea journey of ten days into the arms of my grandfather, hoping he would notice my Wrangler dungarees and new high-top, black, genuine American Converse sneakers. Soon I would be wearing, just like all the other boys around me, linen shorts and blue leather sandals with triangular holes. My home was now the Via Egiziaca, my grandparents' street, the only home of summer I had ever known. Within an hour I was talking and walking and moving my hands just like Peppino from the other side of the courtyard, or at least I thought I was.

The pathway to discovering what this city meant to me had already begun years before, but it remained blurred and confused like vision through a wet window. For now, I only wanted to venture out of my grandparents' house, out of their courtyard and experience this new world I had been thrust into.

I was ten on that summer vacation in Naples, in 1965; and it was the tenth summer I was spending there with my mother's family. My mother, older brother, two-year-old sister, and I had just made another trip to Italy by ship. As usual, my father would fly over to meet us later in the summer. My grandfather, Max, or "Nonno," as I called him, was getting ready to go out with me. He had been up since six, just as he was every morning. Had been smelling the small, crusty rolls on the table all morning while nonchalantly eyeing my krap-fen, a large, sugar-covered, doughy doughnut that gave me a good reason to get up early every day that summer. Krapfen is a German word. The Germans introduced them to Naples while they were conquering it.

I was grateful for this culinary reminder of past con-quest, as krapfens could rarely be found in other cities; the only ones I had seen elsewhere were in Rome, where they were not greasy enough and were too hard. The brown, slick-with-grease bag summoned my morning ambition and the doughnut was quickly made breakfast, along with a tablespoon of coffee in hot milk. Nothing in Naples is bad, even for children, as long as it is diluted enough. A glass of wine with enough water is considered good for an infant's digestion.

As my grandfather and I left the building, we were sur-rounded by the sweet scent of jasmine. The plant overhung my great-aunt's second-story apartment as a greeting to all entering and leaving the courtyard. According to one ac-count, a brother who died in the war had left a small cutting from one of his own plants. It had grown to become this now impressive specimen.

In a few dozen steps, we exited the courtyard. Walking under an arch 30 feet high, we stepped with anticipation into the street, the Via Egiziaca a Pizzofalcone, its cobblestones shiny and smooth from age, its graphite gray and slippery. We had to walk downhill. Like most streets in this neighbor-hood, it turned to new vistas and meandered unevenly, so we could not see the end.

Naples is a city of hills, and each hunched neighborhood has streets that hug its slopes and open up to the streets below, much like small estuaries finding their river. Just a few steps down the street, Giuseppino was sitting in his wicker chair, straw hat askew, his arms folded over the backrest. As always, the door to his house was half-open to the outside. He surveyed the goings-on of the street, examining each passerby as if watching for a thief. This could be a wonderful job, I told myself.

"Roberto, come here," he said.

"Yes?"

"I see you are out with Grandpa. How was your trip from America?"

"Very good. I came on a ship," I replied with pride.

"Oh, that's nice," he said. "Now, I have a question for you. You must explain to me one important thing."

"Yes, what is it?"

"I've heard that in America you have no cheese. How come?"

"But that's not true," I protested. "We have lots of cheese. All kinds."

"I've heard otherwise. Are you sure, Roberto?"

"Yes, I'm positive. Every kind," I repeated for emphasis.

"Okay then, have fun with Nonno. You're positive about the cheese, then, eh?"

"Positive."

"Very good, then. Bye-bye."

As we continued our walk, I noticed that to the left and to the right there were little boys and girls, maybe five or six years old, running along beside me, naked. I tried to look discreetly at the girls with the same bemused stare that I fashioned for any mildly interesting street scene, as if looking at exotic flowers in a pot. It was a difficult task to take in the necessary sights without revealing any interest beyond the ordinary. I did manage to observe a small slit on the little girl, but not much else. Meanwhile, the little boys were dashing about as their little thingies turned around like clock hands gone mad.

A few more feet, a right turn on Via Gennaro Serra, and we would descend down an even steeper road toward the majestic Piazza Plebiscito. There were occasional squeaks from pulleys that rolled out the day's laundry to be dried. Shirts and pants, bras and panties were lined up neatly on a rope and were hanging over our heads, limp vestments from a secret life just beyond the window.

This scene was common in many neighborhoods; a few feet of street was claimed as part of one's dominion. This street also had a bread shop, a small candy store, a tobacco shop where you could buy salt and playing cards, and a barbershop—a rarity. (Where did people get haircuts?)

After passing by some more lines of underwear, we arrived at Donna Carolina's shop, a few feet of space carved out of the building's stone. Donna Carolina was a small, slightly hunchbacked woman dressed in black. She appeared to be 100 years old and no more than 4 ½ feet tall. She seemed to have come with the building, a human gargoyle who hadn't ventured out of that space since Mussolini's march on Rome.

Donna Carolina stood behind a curtain in a window whose wooden shutters opened out along the sides of the building. From this window her head poked out, surveying the street for customers. I was looking for a ring for my cousin, Paola, age four, and Donna Carolina had everything. She ruled over her small dominion with precision and pride.

Here, one could find books, plates, toys of all sorts, pencils, regular pens, pens with pictures of naked women, pots and pans, T-shirts, office supplies, watches, telephones, pocketbooks, pocketknives, handkerchiefs, silverware, various trinkets, dolls, cheap cameras, bedsheets, mugs with scenes of Naples, nativity scene paperweights with snow, and plastic statues of Jesus. Everyone knew that one could buy here with confidence.

I confidently asked for a diamond ring. Nonno was not part of the transaction but was merely a spectator, waiting patiently for me to conduct my business with her. She asked me for a few specifics so she could make a final selection for presentation.

What size, how big, how much did I wish to spend? Apparently these treasures came in the 20-to-50-lire price range (three to seven cents). This was an important decision for me, and I finally settled on the 30-lire version.

Like the Wizard of Oz, she retreated behind the curtain. What wonders must have loomed there—a virtual warehouse of commodities in a few feet of space—indeed, as exacting a use of space as a Mercury capsule! She soon emerged with the desired object affixed to a small piece of cardboard. As if anticipating my only anxiety, she assured me that this ring was adjustable and would fit any size finger. I carefully inspected it and found it to be acceptable.

Pleased that I had made a wise purchase and that I had obviously gotten Donna Carolina's day off to a good start, I turned to look for Nonno so that we could continue our journey. He was talking to the spazzino, the street sweeper. The quick, deliberately rhythmical back-and-forth of the man's long straw broom was mesmerizing. He was like an orchestra conductor, precise and deliberate, playing a mysterious, undetectable melody.

My grandfather was engaging him by telling one of his many jokes—I'd heard each one dozens of times—while the sweeper continued to go about his work. As he posed and rested on his broom an instant, Nonno threw him a cigarette, which he caught and appreciatively accepted. Cigarettes were a precious gift in those days; tobacconists sold them individually in order to obtain even higher profits.

Getting to Piazza Plebiscito, a mere two blocks from our starting point, was no mean accomplishment, since navigating the crowded streets was a challenge. Important decisions had to be made along the way without any hesitation. Should we stop and speak with Antonio? (We had done so the day before); listen to Anna's tales of domestic woe? (Her daughter had run off with a shoe salesman); simply nod to Arturo? (Need we hear about his slipped disc again?); discuss the lack of business with the jeweler? (Why doesn't anyone buy jewelry in the summer?).

Arriving at the Piazza Plebiscito brought a sense of liberation from the routine gazes, inquisitions, and seductions of the busy street. The Piazza was enormous, ¼ mile squared, open to the sky, flanked on one end by a church and on the other by the royal palace. It had at different times been a parking lot, a bus terminal, and an open pedestrian mall, which thousands of pigeons had made their home. With each change there was talk of improvement—this in a city where little improved, where progress was measured in teaspoons.

And invariably conversations turned to talk of improvement. "Finally, someone has had the good sense to get the cars out of the Piazza." The following year it was a parking lot again.

The pattern of apparent renewal repeated itself everywhere. "More bus lines have been added. The buses now have a schedule. The parks have been cleaned up. The train station has clearer signs. The port is open to traffic to ease congestion. The airport has new parking facilities."

Then the improvements melted away, victims of a conspiracy of equilibrium. The parks were dirty again; new signs had been vandalized; the port was closed to traffic; the airport parking lot was full of vendors selling clay pots.

Complaints abounded about every aspect of the city, particularly its seeming anarchy; yet there was a fierce pride in its eccentricities and its resistance to change. Violent discussions erupted at home, between friends, while watching the news, about every aspect of public life. "The strikes are killing us. The cost of everything goes up. You can't catch a bus that isn't packed. The garbage piles up for days. The dogs roam the streets. No one pays a fair share of taxes. Every politician is corrupt."

Complaining, it seemed, was a moral imperative.

Whenever I went to Piazza Plebiscito, I thought of my mother's story. Here, before the war, she had seen Mussolini and Hitler in a car waving to the crowd. When the cars went by, Hitler raised his arms to the cheering crowd. Although everyone was cheering, my mother was not pleased and looked away. A policeman nodded at my mother in approval because he didn't like the Nazis either.

Behind the church from where we had emerged into the Piazza, the snakelike streets sloped upward and ended on precipices that offered a panoramic view of the bay. In front of us, to the side of the Royal Palace, one could look down over a wrought iron railing at the port. As I looked down to see if any ships were in port, I was disappointed. There were none, just small sailboats sprinkled throughout the harbor. White smoke issued from smokestacks in the direction of Vesuvius. On clear days, Sorrento, 15 miles across the bay, was easily visible. To its right was Capri. To me Capri was a giant lying on his back with his knees pointing up; on other days I saw different shapes.

The city had a powerful visual exuberance and I remember thinking how many objects reminded me of things that they were not; the grills of the Fiat 600 appeared to resemble benign, smiling mice.

On this particular day I witnessed a car accident. Two small Fiats collided not too far from where we were walking. The drivers got out slowly, solemnly surveying the damage to each vehicle, looking at each other and wondering who would be the first to speak. At last one of the men, as if to get a ceremony under way, brought the five fingers of his right hand together and moved them up slowly, deliberately, toward his forehead, as if to say, "What were you thinking? Are you an idiot? Have you lost your mind?"

The response was swift and determined. Five other fingers went as high as the arm stretched, not satisfied with merely the comparative, but aiming at once for the superlative. There was a banging on hoods and kicking of doors and admonitions to the gods above. Soon a spiraling verbal barrage was released from both participants, with insults worthy of wartime combatants.

Eventually, both of these gentlemen's families had been duly insulted, including extended members. The seemingly choreographed encounter, a high-pitched opera of sorts, a show of bravado, continued for several minutes. I was momentarily frightened until I looked at those who had gathered to see this free show. Some had put their packages down; a few pushed their way to the front to see better; others had apparently taken this brief interlude as a welcome respite from the day's troubles.

The witnesses' faces were bemused, expectant, and in a few cases even joyous. If the drama's opening scene had been a crescendo, so its final scene was a diminuendo. The curtain finally came down when the two former belligerents shook hands. In one of the damaged cars, a woman sat through the last few minutes of the ordeal clipping her nails, waiting for matters to wind down. Finally the spectators picked up their wares and dispersed, going about their business.

Nonno and I then passed in front of the Royal Palace, several blocks long, four or five stories high, a repetitive series of arches, columns, and windows. There was grandeur and sublimity in this duplication of effect, like the sound of lap-ping waves against rocks. In later years I would think of this building when I heard the phrase, "The corridors of power." There were so many corridors here, and thus there must have been much power.

It seemed, from the outside at least, that all the rooms must have been exactly the same, that the king did not need so many of the same rooms, and that he had simply done it this way to show off. I knew something, even at ten, about show-offs. I had visited Versailles a few years before, another show-off's house.

A few guards always stood in front of this palace, pacing, their only thought seeming to be, "Is it ever going to be lunchtime?"

As we passed the Royal Palace, we were headed to the Galleria, a kind of mall where Michelangelo or Leonardo might have done his Christmas shopping. In front of it was one of the many improvised parking lots, carved out of any available space. A small bulge in a street made a fine three-Fiat 600, or five-Vespa, parking lot. Sidewalks were rare; they were a waste for mere pedestrians when a few cars and Lambrettas could be squeezed into the street. Self-appointed "parking attendants" hovered nearby to direct the intricate maneuvers needed to get into tight spots. They all had white caps that read simply, "Parking Supervisor," and for 500 lire (80 cents) they would watch over your car the entire day.

Approaching the Galleria, we passed in front of the Opera House, the San Carlo. From the outside it was unimposing. I had never been inside but had heard of its splendor. Many stories were connected with this place. My great-aunt Yolanda—my grandmother's sister—had performed here when Mussolini was hosting Hitler in Naples.

As I looked back to find Nonno, he pointed to a window. "Roberto, look there. That's where your father worked after the war. He slept in that room. That's where the English officer's club was."

Then, "The Borboni built this opera house. Isn't it beautiful?"

I wasn't certain that the opera house was beautiful, but I knew what the right answer was. "Yes, molto bello," I said.

It was only years later that I realized my grandfather was referring to "Bourbons," not to "barbarians." In 1734 Cador de Borbon, son of Philip V of Spain, conquered Naples and thus the house of Bourbon was established in Italy. The latter part of the eighteenth century is considered a "golden age" in Neapolitan history.

The enclosed Galleria had four arched entrances, over 30 feet high. Each entrance was at one end of a hallway leading to the central rotunda, topped by a cupola as high as 60 or 70 feet. The floors were marble with inlaid, intricate designs. Thousands of glass panes made up the ceiling. Inside were shops, restaurants, and cafés.

It was much cooler inside than outside, and a faint echo could be heard, the kind found in gymnasiums or nearly empty train stations. On the side we had entered there once stood a movie theater owned by my great-uncle Mario Recanati, back in 1900. It had been the first movie theater in Naples.

In the central rotunda of the Galleria, small groups of men were engaged in conversations, many animated. Most men were wearing well-tailored suits, their arms not in the sleeves but protruding from their jackets. Their white shirts were too tight and between the buttons small blobs of skin tried to pop out. The hands gesticulated in all directions, fingers came together in twos and fours, banging against the head, pounding against the chest, or pointing upward.

I could catch only morsels of conversations as we walked by. "My brother-in-law eats like a horse and sleeps..." "...Yes, you are right to assume everyone is a crook.... "...an ass like two watermelons." One man was involved in a violent diatribe, saying it was time for the goalie at the previous day's soccer game to be sent into exile before any harm came to him. One could not have imagined that Cicero could have spoken more convincingly.

Nonno asked me if I needed anything to drink, since we had been "working" so hard.

"Yes," I said, and we walked into a bar. Unlike what Americans think a bar is, a bar in Italy was where one ate snacks, and drank coffee or soft drinks. Most had marble floors and lots of glass, chrome, and glitz. This one was from another era—ornate, subdued, a remnant of the belle epoch, a backdrop for one of those hokey musicals where women wear hoop skirts and twirl parasols.

We gave our order to the cashier, a young woman sitting on a small podium enclosed in a box. She handed us a slip of paper and my grandfather took it, carefully slipped two ten lire coins (three cents) on it, and put it on the counter. "One coffee and one sixty lire ice cream," he said.

Behind the counter, a man was washing a glass by twirling it under water, a technique that, much to my regret, I later learned involved more skill than was apparent. I tried it twice, both times smashing the glass in my grandma's sink.

The man brought us our items, picked up the coins, and flung them into a dish overflowing with the day's silver booty. Then, without breaking rhythm, he returned to cleaning glasses. Ice creams came in different sizes, from 20 to100 lire (three to fifteen cents). Great care was required to get out the right amount of ice cream, since the same-sized scooper was used for all requests. It was a feat comparable to those attendants at Horn and Hardart, who would dig twenty nickels out of their apron pockets in one clean swoop for your dollar.

One twirl of the wrist into the silver basin and out came 60 or 80 or 100 lire worth of hazelnut ice cream. No matter which bar you went to, the correct amounts were placed on your cone, certainly the result of a conspiracy of ice-cream servers, a skill of exact measurement too astounding to be the result of mere chance. Apparently they had all gone to the same bar "college."

With a quick goodbye, we left the bar and the Galleria and emerged onto Via Roma, or the Via Toledo, as some called it. This was the main shopping area, in previous times one of the most renowned in Europe, the street I always had to see first to confirm my arrival. It was not Vesuvius or the bay that was the hallmark of Naples to me but the familiar shops on this street.

They were the same every year, displaying wares with the touch of an artist, landmarks of many summers, a comforting assertion of the continuity of life. There was the photo shop with rolls of neatly displayed new and used cameras, ladies' handbags arranged in semicircles, summer shoes held in a fishnet, and obelisks of newspapers and toys. On the obelisks the papers hung 8 feet high from the ground at 45-degree angles, with only the headlines showing. On the other side were the toys, in the summer mostly pails and shovels, arranged by color and size. Aesthetic appeal was paramount in every display.

The street, nevertheless, was not too elegant for a fruit vendor. Peaches, apricots, and cherries were arranged in order of size in boxes slightly tilted, bouquets of summer fruit.

The beggars were out too, each in the same spot as always, as predictable as the presence of fire hydrants. Many of the mendicant women would sit barefoot on the ground with little children around them. Infants were rented out to beggars, and those with missing limbs or visible deformities brought premium prices.

We passed one beggar, partially blind, who was sitting in a wooden folding chair, wearing a gray suit and a tie. He leaned on a small wooden table bearing a dish to accept donations. Nonno gave him a coin and in return received a slip of paper on which was written, "Thank you very much: Truly, Professore Barese." A small placard rested by his feet with his "office hours." As he thanked us after we had dropped the coin, he announced that he would be on vacation for three weeks starting the following Monday and that his brother would be in his spot to fill in.

We next had to stop to get a letter stamped and mailed. The main post office building, just off Via Roma, was a prime example of fascist architecture: immense, solid, monumental, all stone and marble. The grand stairs leading to the main entrance seemed worthy of a coronation, overexuberantly regal for the present-day purpose of mailing a letter.

We resumed our walk. A few streets down, Nonno stopped in front of a man who was stretching a piece of cloth over the seat of a chair. He asked him if Luigi was inside. The man said, "Yeah, go inside." Nonno told me to come with him, but I wanted to stay out in the street and watch the workers.

"Okay," he said. "Wait here while I talk to Luigi. I'll be out in a minute."

I walked a few paces down the block and came to a doorway covered only in thin, hanging, plastic strips of yellow and green and red, common in bars and pastry shops. From inside, a dark, reddish light was glowing and I could hear faint laughter and the intermittent high-pitched voices of women.

Pushing a few plastic strips aside, I walked in. In front of me were two red velvet couches, one facing me and the other with its back to the door. On the one facing me a woman was sitting, wearing a silk nightgown and a pair of high-heeled red slippers with feathers. On the other couch I could make out a man's back, a sailor in uniform, his white hat dangling sideways. A woman was on his lap, sipping a drink from a straw. The man turned around, looked at me briefly, and said in a southern accent, "Hey, boy. Wuts you duin' here?"

I couldn't move, out of fear. A woman approached from behind a counter; she was well-rounded, in high, red heels. I couldn't make her out in the dark.

"Bring the stuff here, boy," she yelled out. I was still silent, unable to move. "Well?" she called out "Bring it here. Hey, are you the delivery boy from the bar?"

"No," I managed to say. She approached, wearing nothing on top. Her breasts were large, meaty, and hanging, forming a large crease where they rested against her body. As she approached, I looked away from her large breasts, as if they were as common to me as houseflies in summer. "What do you want here?" she demanded.

"Oh, nothing," I said, wanting to stay and to run at the same time. I managed finally to turn around and within what seemed like a second I was out on the street again, looking for Nonno. I didn't dare tell him about the woman with the big breasts for fear that I had done something wrong by seeing her.

After I found him, he announced that he would get a cappuccino and then we would be on our way. We then started to walk back home, almost retracing the same route we had previously taken.

The sun was blazing, reflecting off chrome car bumpers and the windshields of Lambrettas and Vespas. The shutters soon came down on the stores, which would remain closed until four o'clock when the heat would begin its retreat. After lunch it seemed that everyone slept for two hours, and the city fell silent.

By following a walkway along one of the city's many tunnels, we came to an elevator, one of many where, upon paying three cents, we were invited in. It was large, dark, and cavernous, but "worth it" because it saved us a lot of walking up the steep streets.

We then walked to the "special" bus stop to "do the climb."

A unique, extra small bus that went to the Monte Di Dio Street—needed for the narrow streets—came this way every half hour or so, depending on lunch breaks, the family situation of the driver, and the alignment of Jupiter's moons, it seemed. This was the last stop before "the climb." Taking the bus here cost three cents rather than the usual seven. A bus came surprisingly soon and we got on.

The ticket man was sitting on a raised platform in the back with tickets of tissue-thin white paper, which he gave to us with a masterful stroke of his arm, peeling off two 20-lire ones and handing them to us in one graceful motion. He was wearing a gray uniform and a leather pouch, from which he pulled out change.

I sat down, noticing that there was a commotion up front. A small crowd had gathered outside the bus and some men behind me rushed to the front door. They were pulling a woman's arms. The bus driver got out of his seat and started pulling as well.

"Lady, your fat ass is stuck in my door."

"Why do they make these doors so small?"

"This ain't the Royal Palace. It's just a bus."

In the meantime, some men from the street were trying to push her in. "The cork is stuck in the bottle," someone shouted.

"You guys are having a good time back there, eh? My brother-in-law would pay good money to do what you're doing," the lady yelled out.

"This ain't no fun, lady. This ass is as ripe as a rotten melon. Maybe about ten years ago this might have been fun."

"Grease her up. She'll fly outta there like a cork from a New Year's Eve champagne bottle," a man behind me called out.

The commotion finally subsided and the lady got in. Two men, who were sitting next to each other, got up, bowed to her, and offered their seats.

"I know you guys had a good time," she said, sitting down with a huff.

Even after the bus ride, there was a small "climb" remaining before we got home. We entered the courtyard. The dulcet song of wind through leaves filled the air. Bees were circling the jasmine plant, making the sound of torpid, Neapolitan afternoons.

Pasquale, the concierge, greeted me, asking what adventures I had experienced.

"So many," I said.

Maria, the housekeeper, asked, "Where have you been?"

"To the port and the Piazza Plebiscito," I told her.

"Gesu, Gesu! It's so dangerous there," she yelled out.

"Did you enjoy going to work with Nonno?" my grandmother called out.

"Work? Nonno has a job?" I asked with great confusion.

Yes, Nonno had a job, I learned. He sold materials to upholsterers, and I had just accompanied him on one of his busy days.

There were many more walks to come in the next two summers and many more "busy" workdays for Nonno and me. His love for the city, his love for the people he talked with, as well as his jokes, never changed. He passed away in 1968, and at that moment, a vital breath that had sustained the life of Naples and its people was extinguished for me as well.

When Nonno died, an era of my life was coming to a close, but the story of my summers in Naples and how meaningful they were for me began many years before.

Chapter Two

—∞—

Revelation in Ischia

Ischia is one of the islands in the bay, a little closer to the port of Naples than Capri and larger than that "sister island," but geographically less defined. Its coastline gently slopes upward to the center of the island, where a steep incline forms a mountain topped by the cone of an extinct volcano. Hot water springs and beaches line the coastline while pine trees and brush blanket the interior.

One day in 1961 I went there with my father. We got off the little ferry to a blazing, morning sun. A man was pulling sliced coconut out of ice water to entice buyers at a penny a piece as eager tourists thumped down the plank. A sailor called out, "Last return is at 7 P.M. If you miss it, you're stuck here." A few men were standing around holding up signs written out on pieces of cardboard.

A small boy ran over to us, not much older than I, and pulled on my father's sleeve. "You like good hotel? Vieni."

My father said, "No, thank you," as he strained his eyes in the sunlight trying to find something or someone. Suddenly a tall, blonde woman in a long white dress came out of a crowd and extended her hand like a rudder. "Leo, here you are," she said.

"This is Robert," my father replied. "Hello!"

As we walked to an open car with a high straw roof braced by four bamboo posts, I wondered, *Who is this blonde woman?* I didn't know my father knew any women besides my mother and relatives. And if he did know other women, shouldn't they be old and ugly?

I looked casually out of the car at all the people in sandals and bathing suits. After a few minutes' drive, we got to the courtyard of a hotel. My father, the lady, the driver, and I got out and stepped onto a pavement made of blue tiles with tiny yellow suns painted right in the middle. Two large potted plants stood on each side of the doorway to the hotel. To one side in the distance, through the swaying branches and leaves of a fig tree, I could see the water, perfectly blue except for a few lines of white sunlight.

"Let's go to our room," my father said. "Then we will eat something."

The room was large, with gold furniture carved of wood and a ceiling higher than a museum's. Soon it was time to eat, and in the dining room the blonde lady sat with us for a few minutes. She left, then came back and started talking to my father, who had finished his meal and was standing next to her.

I was still eating ice cream, but my father was involved in conversation with the woman, and I began to worry about what had to be done next. Should I leave a tip? There were thick curtains on the windows and waiters in white suits and gloves. This looked like the kind of place where waiters expected tips. Did I have any money on me? Yes, I had an American nickel. Could I leave a nickel in Italy? Yes, the waiter could go to a bank and change it into Italian money.

I was very confused and uncomfortable. I finished eating and pulled out the nickel and placed it by my plate. I was waiting for the blonde woman to comment about how knowledgeable I was about tipping, but she laughed instead. Had I left too much? Had I left too little? Was it wrong to leave American money?

That night, as the sun set and clouds hung in the sky over the bay, an orange blanket lay over the island and the crickets settled down to sing. The darkness crept into the pine trees and then leapt up to chase the light away. Lying in bed next to my father, I wanted to ask him, "Who is that woman?" But instead I said, "Where did you meet Mommy?"

"I met her here in Italy after the war." I had heard of the war but didn't know what it was. I would have to find out more about it, I thought. I was falling asleep when my father said, "Do you see how dark it is in this room? You can't see anything. In a few minutes you will be able to see."

"Why will I be able to see?"

"Your eyes will adjust to the dark. Just wait."

I waited for a while until I could see the outline of a jacket hanging on a chair. Back home I would cover my face as the reflection of car lights moving on the ceiling frightened me. Now, the jacket was scaring me. I imagined that a man was sitting in the jacket about to turn around and lunge for me at any moment.

"Can you see anything yet?"

"I can see the jacket on the chair and a little bit of the chair too," I whispered.

In a little while I could see lots of things. Eyes adjust to the darkness. The sun makes light. The darkness is a magic blanket that wipes the light away. I fell asleep.

—m—

"Wake up," my father said. "We have lots to do. How did you sleep?"

"Hey, it's morning."

"Yes, it's morning," he confirmed patiently.

"No. It's really morning. Not like back home."

"What do you mean?"

"Back home it's the middle of the day already, no matter when I wake up. The trucks and cars are making noise and it doesn't feel like morning."

"Let's get up. We have a long day ahead."

We first went to a beach full of pebbles near the "fungo," where a mushroomlike rock sticks out of the water. By squirming and pushing my way into the tiny, smooth rocks, I could make a comfortable bed contoured to my body. A few rocks sizzled on different parts of my skin. As I pressed my ear down, I could hear a slight whisper of air moving through the rocks. What was it trying to say?

"Daddy," I asked again, "Where did you meet Mommy and when did you meet her?"

"I met her in Naples after the war. After the war I went to look for my brother in Italy and I met Mommy. You know about the numbers on my arm. I got them in a concentration camp. After the concentration camp, that's when I came here. Later we moved to New York."

I was silent for a while, thinking. Things were starting to make sense. During the war my father hadn't known my mother. He was at a constipation camp where they drew numbers on him, probably to be sure who belonged to the constipation camp and who didn't. After he got tired of the camp he left it and started looking for his brother, who was swimming in Italy because the swimming was not as good in Germany. My father got tired of swimming in Italy and he then went to America, where there was less swimming but there were other things like baseball and smooth toilet paper and milk that you could drink.

Walking back along the side of the road, on one of the many steep climbs that led from the beach to the hotel, we saw a small store with fruits. "Look at these huge figs," I called out. They were the purple-skinned ones, the "early" ones, as everyone called them, those that were not supposed to be as good. But they tasted the same to me as the more prestigious, green-skinned ones.

My father and I walked in to buy a bagful. A hunched-over woman less than 3 feet tall came from a back room and asked if she could be of any help. My father said, "We would like two kilos of figs and also some hazelnuts."

"How many hazelnuts?"

"About 500 lire worth" (80 cents).

The woman placed figs in a bag and weighed them. She then disappeared into the back room, this time returning with an enormous jar, half her size, filled with hazelnuts. She held it carefully, as if it were a sick child, and placed the jar on the counter. A sign was taped on the jar, "Hazelnuts, 10 lire each."

With a surgeon's precision, she placed her hand inside the jar, felt around with her fingers and pulled one hazelnut out as she said, "And that makes ten," placing it quietly on the counter. "I am picking out the big ones for you."

She put her hand in again, felt around once more, and came out with a large one. "And that makes twenty," she said, placing the hazelnut neatly alongside the first. Her hand went in and out of the jar in slow deliberate strokes, "pianissimo"; the woman was conducting the "Hazelnut Symphony." The hazelnuts were lined up straight and evenly spaced, like soldiers in training. Mesmerized by the slow-moving arm, the soft song of a cricket outside the store, and the numb feeling that comes after sun and swimming, I almost fell asleep.

I could see my father's eyes following the arc of the woman's hand and inspecting each hazelnut to make sure it was a perfect one. Then, as if to break his trance, he called out,

"Enough" with the conviction of a tortured prisoner deciding to tell all he knows.

"But it is only 340 lire worth, sir."

"Yes, thank you. That will do."

As we left the store, I asked my father, "Did you want to get out of there in a hurry?"

"Yes," he said. "At least before a new pope is picked."

"Why were you at a constipation camp?" I asked him, surprising even myself.

"No, no, no. It was a *concentration* camp. I was there because I was a Jew."

"And what did you do there?"

"It was a terrible place where many people were worked to death and killed. I lost most of my family there."

I did not want to know any more. I wanted to cover my ears and shut out any more words and pull out the words that had already gone in. Fortunately, there weren't any more words; the only sound was of our footsteps and the distant barking of a dog. At first the interruption of conversation was liberating, but slowly feelings of confusion and pain filled the silence.

I concentrated on the sound of the barking dog and the laughter of two people sitting on a doorstep as we walked by. I thought of the woman putting hazelnuts on the counter, how she counted them with precision, how serious she had been about her job, how her concentration must have pushed back the world just a little bit from squeezing in around her.

My father pointed ahead to a small clearing in the thick bushes. "Look, here we are. This is the path that leads to the hotel."

—m—

Over the years I would acquire more pieces of the story until there was a fairly consistent narrative about what had happened during the war and how my father ended up in Naples.

He had been born in 1922 in Bautzen, a small, medieval German town. A few years later he moved to Breslau, which after the war was in Poland. His immediate family consisted of his mother, father, and four brothers. The family was wealthy and had a maid, a nanny, a cook, and a driver. My grandfather owned a furniture factory, some stores, and real estate in several cities. Despite the rising torrent of anti-Semitism and the increasing brutality of the Nazi regime in the 1930s, the family hoped to ride out the storm and never considered emigrating; the eldest brother, however, went to Palestine at age eighteen, fortunately never to return.

After the Jewish-owned businesses were "Aryanized" and property and valuables were seized, my father's family, except for himself and a younger brother, was suddenly taken away to a ghetto and then sent to Sobibor, an extermination camp. Here, my father would later learn, his parents and one brother were killed immediately upon arrival.

Unaware of the fate of his family, my father continued to work while surreptitiously obtaining counterfeit French travel documents that allowed some French laborers to return to France on leave.

One day my father decided to escape with his younger brother, Kurt, using one of the forged travel papers. He was betrayed just as he was about to board a train for France. Following his arrest, he was tried for obtaining false identities, and my father and others were forced to testify about their clandestine activities. In order to spare Kurt a harsh sentence, my father testified to his innocence, hoping this would shield him from harsh punishment.

Kurt was acquitted, but with tragic consequences: He wasn't sent to prison but taken to Auschwitz because he was a Jew.

My father, on the other hand, was convicted and sent to a normal prison in another city. One day, the jail keeper called him over. "Hey, you Jew," he said, "What are you doing in my beautiful prison? You do not belong here."

That day, a car brought my father back to Breslau, where he was put in a dark, crowded cellar where he shared use of an overflowing pail full of feces and urine. The others were hardened criminals and political prisoners. Since there was no room in the cell to stretch out his body, he had to sleep in an upright position. Once he was even hit on the head with a pipe—the dent is still there, and my father has rubbed my hand across it to feel the concave contour of his skull.

Eventually he was brought in a special prisoners' railroad car to Auschwitz. The starvation (each day he was given only some water in a tin cup and a piece of "sawdust bread"), the physical and mental torture, the constant presence of death, the total lack of hope, and the knowledge that the family was probably destroyed—how could this be endured? For those fortunate enough not to be put to death immediately upon entering the camp, it took only one insignificant gesture—a look in one direction rather than in the other, one word rather than another—that meant the difference between life and death.

Upon entering the camp, my father found a friend, a gentile who had worked with him on obtaining the forged papers. He too was a prisoner but was responsible for other inmates as well. He secured a job for my father in the laundry service, which meant refuge from the cold and therefore better chances for survival.

Besides the life-and-death tightrope to be walked, three quotes from his fellow prisoners stood out in my father's recitation of events. One was advice given to him early on in the camp. "Do not look right or left; look straight ahead." To be robotized was often preferable to being singled out for an imaginary offense.

Another was a prisoner's paraphrasing of Dante's words at the gates of hell: "Abandon all hope, ye who enter." Like Dante, the victims in the camp were in hell, but without a guide and with no hope of reemerging to live beneath the stars in freedom.

The third was the vestige of humor that managed to survive in the Frenchman who announced the menu for each evening's meal, before the sawdust arrived. "As an appetizer, you may choose beluga caviar or escargots or a selection of fresh fruits. As a main dish, beef bourguignon with carrots Lorraine or pheasant under glass in a light orange sauce..."

As the Allies were approaching, the camp had to be abandoned and thus began the long and infamous Death March out of the camp. Prisoners were forced to walk in treacherous snow wearing only their striped prison uniforms in the middle of winter. Those who could not walk were shot on the spot; others simply took their last breath and fell in the snow. After days of marching, the column of the half-dead arrived at a camp, from which they were transferred to other concentration camps.

My father was sent to Dachau, but after several months Dachau also had to be abandoned because of the approaching Allied forces. The inmates were put on a train to be taken away, and my father was shoved into a crowded open car. Somewhere along the way he leaned off the side as if he were about to defecate. The train turned around a bend and my father suddenly saw his opportunity. He jumped backward into the snow and lay there until the train had disappeared. When he got up, he saw that he was in a field. Miraculously, he found a hunter's cabin, where he hid for several days. During the night he would leave the cabin and dig small potatoes out of the ground. This was the diet that kept him barely alive. He hung on, day to day, living only for the moment that his rescuers might arrive.

One day he heard the rumble of armor moving on a nearby road. Near-dead from typhus and delirious, weighing ninety pounds despite being five feet ten inches, he knew this was his last chance—he would either live or die right here. He staggered toward a column of soldiers and, to his intense relief, saw that they were American. Tears of joy streamed down his face as he moved unsteadily toward them.

Could his ordeal actually be coming to an end? His joy was mixed with sadness so deep that he could not imagine it ever leaving him. His parents, two younger brothers, grandparents, and uncles, aunts, and cousins were all dead. And by some miracle, he had lived.

"I am greeting my liberators," he said to his rescuers in halting English. The soldiers stopped, staring at the emaciated, hollow-eyed man before them in disbelief. "Why are you in this condition? Who are you?"

"I am a Jew and I have been in a camp," he told them, tears pouring down his cheeks. Upon hearing those words, one of the men, a Jewish chaplain, pulled out a prayer book and asked my father to read it. He took the book in shaking hands and read a few lines of a Hebrew prayer. Looking up anxiously, he saw an expression of pure compassion on the chaplain's face.

"We must bring this man to the nearby house for food," he told the other soldiers. Hurriedly, they half-carried my father to a home now occupied by several women.

"Take care of this man," they were ordered, and they followed those orders. My father remained with them for several days, in near delirium, after which he was sent to a displaced person's camp. There he stayed for several weeks, battling surges of nausea and stomach cramps. He could take in only small amounts of food, for his stomach had shrunk to almost nothing and could not digest solids. In tiny, gradual steps, he found the food easier to digest until he could eat small amounts without feeling sick. Later he would hear of prisoners, liberated from Auschwitz, who had died because they had eaten too much.

When soldiers from a Jewish brigade came by the camp inquiring about survivors, my father told them that he wanted to locate his brother Sigi, who was with the British Army. When my father found out that one of the soldiers had relatives in Newark, New Jersey, he told the soldier that he too had relatives there. The soldier was able to send a letter that my father had written to his relatives. Within a few days a letter for my father arrived from Newark informing him that Sigi was somewhere in Italy, but it could give no more specific details.

My father insisted on trying to get to Italy despite the advice of the soldiers of the brigade, who felt him to be too frail to make the journey. They finally agreed to get him across the border to Italy, but he was to lie low in an army transport truck. If they were stopped, he was to feign sleep and remain silent.

He succeeded in crossing the border and went to Jewish Brigade Headquarters in northern Italy. There he was peppered with questions, for he was the first concentration camp survivor anyone there had seen. "Are Jews really being slaughtered, as was rumored?" he was asked. Despite knowing some of the horrors of the camps, the brigade members seemed stunned to hear about them in such detail.

His new friends then gave my father a list of places in Italy where British soldiers from Palestine were stationed. He was given a pass as an employee of the British Army and was allowed to ride on British army vehicles. That meant that, if they were to pass by, he could flag them down and hitch a ride to the possible locations where Sigi might be. Thus began a long trip through Italy. He searched in various cities unsuccessfully, making his way from the north of Italy to the south.

Upon arriving in Naples, he went to the Jewish soldiers' club, hoping to find some food. As he was sitting and eating, an officer approached and said, "Excuse me, but there is a soldier in my company who looks exactly like you."

"That's who I'm looking for. It's my brother," my father replied excitedly. "Where is he?"

"Come back tomorrow and your brother will be here," the officer said. "Tonight you can sleep at the Palestinian garrison here in Naples."

The next morning the two brothers were reunited. Running to each other, they joyously embraced. They hadn't seen each other in six years. "I thought you were dead," they said to each other, reluctant to separate from their long embrace.

"How is our family?" my uncle asked.

"I'm not sure, but I fear the worst," my father replied honestly.

My father returned with his brother to the beach where he was stationed. He was given a tent to share with one of the soldiers. One day after roll call my father was informed that the company would be moving on soon and that he could not go with them. He would be lodged in Amalfi, a city on the coast south of Naples, where two women who were paid to supply food and shelter would care for him. There he stayed for three miserable weeks. It was stifling hot and uncomfortable, and the horrors of recent events visited him while he was both asleep and awake.

When Sigi got in touch with him, my father said that he wanted to find some work. At an employment agency in Naples, my father was told to go to the British officers' club in the San Carlo Opera House. Here he could work and sleep. And he did, for eighteen months, until July 1946, when he married my mother and emigrated to America.

The boat ride back to Naples with my father that day in 1961 was not smooth. Clouds had settled over the bay. They were puffy white on the contours but dark gray in the middle. I placed my chin on my hands as I leaned over the wooden plank so that my face caught the wind, and I could look down at the white foam hitting the side of the boat and the waves slapping each other.

I had found out, without drama, the identity of the blonde woman; she was a friend of my father's, the proprietor of the hotel where we were staying. I had also learned more of the war; however, it was something I wanted no part of, at least not then.

At that time there were many things I didn't know, and so many things I didn't want to know. Hearing my father's story in Ischia was the first time I realized how deep the connection was between Naples and my family—and therefore me as well. As I continued to visit my grandparents every summer, I began to form strong bonds with my Neapolitan neighbors.

Chapter Three

— ∞ —

Pasquale

There are people for whom the tragic sense of life, the disappointments of failed dreams, and the absurd machinations of fate bear an especially heavy burden. They face life stoically, breathing in and savoring its joys, and bearing the weight of its injustices with equanimity. For some such people, their stories may be read in their faces, in the lines that droop from the eyes to the ridge below the cheekbones, and especially in the fathomless gaze that tells you that they have seen, if fleetingly, life as a whole. Such a person was my friend Pasquale.

I was a preteen and he was fiftyish, about five feet six inches and heavyset when I knew him in the mid-1960s in Naples. Pasquale was the concierge at my grandmother's house and lived in a small room above a large portico leading to a courtyard. He spent most of his days in this tiny room, where he was well placed to observe the comings and goings of visitors.

His sanctuary contained a small table, two chairs, and a small black-and-white television set. If, when walking by, I would catch him unawares, I would usually find him sitting with his head in his hands, pensively watching his television or simply lost in thought.

Occasionally he would invite me to dinner, which usually consisted of a tomato sandwich. "Tomatoes keep the blood flowing through the head and are a cure for any type of headache," he would tell me, generously dispensing his folk wisdom.

On other nights I would buy us some *sciurilli e panzarotti*, fried dough balls with eggplant, fish, or meat in them at a penny a piece, and we would sit and eat them in the courtyard.

Pasquale had lots of stories to tell, many of them about his wartime exploits—or lack of them. They were perfectly believable because they were mostly tales of his cowardice. For example, he had not even been sure how to use his rifle, but it didn't really matter, as he had never intended to use it anyway.

A raid one day by a single-engine British propeller plane sent him running for his life. "That's when I learned I had an excellent heart," he told me. "I was so frightened and I ran so fast that if I did not drop dead then, I was sure I was going to live many more years."

Pasquale did not understand why there were wars or why there was hate. His ideology extended only to the beauty of nature and the enjoyment of life. One day he invited me to go on a trip with him. When I asked where we were going, he said, "It's a surprise."

I could barely contain my excitement as I walked down to the courtyard from my grandmother's house to his apartment. I found him waiting for me, dressed up better than usual.

We got on his Vespa, of which he was very proud, and drove down the street to a tobacconist's shop, where he bought one cigarette and one piece of gum. Pasquale looked at the cigarette as tenderly as one might regard a newborn baby, then put it in his pocket along with the gum. Obviously this was all part of his grand plan.

We then rode to a park, where the bay was spread out before us in its full, midday splendor. The sunlight danced on the gentle waves and the smell of sea salt filled the air.

"Sit down, Roberto, and look out at the water and the mountains," he urged gently.

I had thought this was just a stop on our way to somewhere else, but no...this was it! This was where he had intended to go all along. The piece of gum slid out of Pasquale's pocket and into my hand. Then the cigarette emerged from his pocket. He held it up to the light to catch one more glimpse before lighting it, and when he took the first puff, his face had the look of breathless anticipation, as if he were a refugee arriving in a free land.

Pasquale was savoring this moment as if it were his last.

I, however, could not participate in the same "spirit of the moment" as my friend. Instead I chewed my gum and looked silently out over the water. My impatience must have been evident from my body language, because Pasquale glanced my way and asked if anything was wrong. I told him that nothing was wrong at all, but deep down I was deeply disappointed that we weren't going to a more exotic location.

The beating of a young boy's heart has a different calling than that of a seasoned man. Only as an adult could I grasp the sense of satisfaction and contentment that comes when desire can no longer be satiated by illusions of progress. Rather, the day comes when solitude and the cessation of needless activity are the true requisites for satisfaction.

"Can anything be better than this?" Pasquale had asked contentedly, leaving the answer to the gentle breeze. The silence worked its way between us, and I stared out over the light shimmering on the water, wondering what he meant.

A more puckish side of Pasquale emerged one day when he learned that a cousin of mine—a woman of about forty—was coming to visit from Torino. She would be sleeping on a straw mattress in a private room that I had been occupying all summer.

The day after she arrived, Pasquale told me he had seen her and that he had a question for me. "Is she sleeping in that straw bed?" he wanted to know.

"Yes," I said, "That's where I've been sleeping in all summer."

He then admitted that he wanted to perform an experiment and wondered if I would help him.

"Of course," I agreed, whereupon he gave me a long piece of string and scissors and asked me to go up to my cousin's room. While I was there, I was to look out the window, and he would give me detailed instructions about what to do next.

I went to the room, an eager collaborator, and leaned out to get instructions.

"Look at the bed and see if there is an obvious indentation." There was. "Lay the string along the indentation, from one end to the other, and cut the string so it is the same length as the indentation. That way we will know how big her ass is. Be precise."

From Pasquale's serious demeanor I took my task to be very important, and I did as he asked. Then, when I came down with the string and the scissors, we went into his little room. He took the cut string, held it up, and examined it as closely as if he were a radiologist looking for a cyst.

"This is truly impressive," he said, "and just what I thought. This beats my wife by quite a bit. As a young intern, I took mental notes in ass measurement. Yes, her ass is truly impressive." Turning to me with a grin, he said, "Roberto, let's cut up a tomato and get some bread for lunch." Then, he repeated to himself, "Yes, truly impressive."

Pasquale was modest and only lightly schooled, but he had an uncanny knack for "reading people." For example, he would tell me about my uncles, aunts, and grandparents, astonishing me with his ability to get to the core of their anxieties and problems. "Your grandmother is an anxious person and is increasingly frustrated because she can't walk after breaking her hip. Your grandfather has trouble facing problems head-on."

After meeting my uncle from Israel, Pasquale sized him up after a brief conversation. "Israel is the right place for your uncle. He is cosmopolitan and needs the stimulus of seeing people from many different parts of the world."

Pasquale once summed up the Cold War by way of salt and pepper shakers. He put them both on a table, then picked them up and hid them behind his back. "That is Russia," he said as he pointed to the empty space where the shakers had been. "Russians will lie and tell you that they have nothing." Then he put the shakers back and took one away. "The United States will tell you that what you see is all they have. They will show you 'A' but they will not show you 'B'. There is not as much difference between both countries as many would believe."

Once, sensing an inner anxiety in me, he called me over and confided that his wife was concerned about a sick relative and had become depressed. He asked if I might suggest something to make her feel better. I came up with a couple of ideas, and he soberly reflected on my suggestions. We then discussed them and together amended them so they might bring comfort to his wife. In doing so, he had made me feel that I had contributed something important, and in the process my anxiety vanished.

Another time, I was worried about my lack of preparedness for my bar mitzvah. While most people simply told me not to worry, that I would do fine, Pasquale took a different approach. He called me over and told me stories about how afraid he had been when he had to take his fourth grade exams. Again, while listening to his own tales of terror, I quickly forgot my own fears.

On the day of my bar mitzvah, it was Pasquale who led the procession of cars to the synagogue, riding his Vespa with sober propriety—although I don't think he actually knew what a bar mitzvah was. During the ceremony Pasquale was moved by the Hebrew prayers, and a tear ran down his check.

Pasquale was not a learned man, but rather than conversing about the things he knew, he wondered about the things he didn't. He respected learning and knowledge in others as if he intuited their importance. He told me that the greatest Italians were the Roman writer Virgil, the medieval writer Dante, and the philosopher Benedetto Croce. While he knew very little of their works, he respected their passion for knowledge. "A great writer must be given the room to let his ideas go where they may," he told me. "A society needs free minds or it will wither and die."

An event one day showed me a new, yet disturbing side of Pasquale's situation. One afternoon Pasquale had to pick up a package in another town. I went along with him on his Vespa. After riding an hour over bumpy roads, we stopped to eat lunch in a small outdoor restaurant. After sitting down, we looked out over the landscape that gently sloped down toward an orchard. When a butterfly landed on the table, we both stared silently at it, appreciating its ephemeral beauty.

"It will die soon," said Pasquale pensively. "Thus it is made more beautiful."

When it was time to order our meal, the waiter, who had apparently seen us pull up and park the Vespa, asked Pasquale about his mode of transportation.

"How come you're driving a Vespa?" he challenged my friend.

"It's convenient and I enjoy the feeling of it. It's fun to drive," responded Pasquale equably.

But the waiter was unrelenting. "I mean, a big man like you, on a Vespa...someone your size needs a car."

Pasquale thought for a second, but the best he could come up with was, "There is a great expense in maintaining a car."

I could see the waiter's look of triumph at Pasquale's weak rejoinder to the thinly disguised insult. He had taken satisfaction in inserting a dagger in the poor man's heart. I was fuming inside. Poor Pasquale—he had suffered total defeat at this idiot's hands. Try as he might, he could not find the proper facade to present to me after being so humiliated. The rest of our ride was mostly silent, both of us in our private worlds.

When we finally arrived back home, it was getting dark. As he got off his Vespa, Pasquale asked if I had had a good time, and I assured him that I had. Later, as I was preparing for bed, I saw a faint light spilling on the step in front of Pasquale's small room. Impulsively, I decided to reassert how much I had enjoyed riding on his Vespa, and I went down to say "good night" again. But when I approached his home, I saw Pasquale sitting with his head in his hands, staring straight ahead, barely visible in a penumbra of dim light.

I had never before noticed how small the room, the chairs, and the table were. Pasquale's body seemed to fill the space so completely that he appeared almost cartoonlike, a man too big for this room. Like an insect in amber, he seemed to be eternally suspended there.

Suddenly distraught, I turned and ran as fast as I could. I needed to get home, and quickly, so I could try to erase those unwanted images of my dear friend, Pasquale.

Chapter Four

You Want to Be Americano?

No matter how easily I slipped into "Naples mode" when I arrived each summer in the streets of *bassi* (street-level apartments) to take up residence, I was always the "Americano." Although I wore the shirts and sandals of the boys on the street, spoke with a tinge of a Neapolitan dialect, ate the same foods, played with the same toys, and wanted the same things all the other boys did on the Via Pizzofalcone, no one was deceived.

In fact, everyone knew that I wasn't from the neighborhood or anywhere near it. The haircut, the accent, the knowledge that I wasn't around the rest of the year gave me away. Everyone in Naples was a *ficcanaso* (one who sticks his nose in things—a busybody), and they knew I was the grandchild from Nuova York.

"Roberto has arrived," someone in my grandmother's building would call out, and word got out fast. Immediately I was pelted with questions. "How was the trip? How long will you stay? You grew a lot this year, more than you did last year."

Our neighbor Mrs. Malvese, peering from her tiny apartment called out, "Another summer, Robertino, welcome.

There will be some life out here now in the courtyard. How are your momma and your dad?"

In the first few excited hours after each arrival, people slowly came out to see me, called from the window, or transmitted greetings through others. The "Americani are here for the summer," I heard someone call from the building.

Maria Teresa, who was my age, lived just below my grandmother. She appeared before me one year just after my arrival, with *tamburrelle*—a set of two tambourine-like drums that hit a small rubber ball back and forth—along with bocce balls. "They're brand-new," she assured me. "Are you too tired to play later today?" Maria Teresa wasn't really interested if I was American or not. She was interested in playing in the courtyard, especially during the afternoon "siesta" when the adults were sleeping.

It may seem unusual that an American boy in the 1960s in an Italian city of over a million people should be such an interesting phenomenon. However, Naples had a different relationship with its tourists and foreigners than did other Italian cities. In Rome, Florence, and Venice, tourists—in those days mostly Americans—came in large numbers and wandered all the neighborhoods and *vicoletti* (little streets). They could be seen taking cabs and sitting in the cafés and restaurants, their Japanese 35-millimeter cameras and Kodak Instamatics dangling from their necks.

American tourists to Italy often avoided Naples altogether, or came from Rome for the day, then went straight to Pompeii or Sorrento. Groups of Americans could be seen huddled in front of the *aliscafi* (hydrofoils) or *vaporetti* (ferry boats) waiting to go to Capri or Ischia. I knew they were American by their brightly colored shirts and blouses.

Other tourists sidestepped Naples because of the *scippatori* (muggers). Most guidebooks advised avoiding Naples altogether or stopping only for the day in order to get to the sites outside the city. Those who insisted on staying were advised to hold tightly to cameras, luggage, and pocketbooks to avoid youths on Vespas who would grab whatever they could.

The sixth fleet was stationed in Naples and the destroyers and aircraft carriers were anchored in the bay. But even the sailors stayed near the port or limited their excursions to a few downtown shopping streets. They usually walked in small groups or in pairs, their white hats easily standing out in crowds.

Besides this local insularity that made me an intriguing and foreign presence, the cult of American power and culture was very marked. The cold war had ideologically divided the world between America and Russia, with Italy in the middle. There were many Communists in the country, but most Italians clearly were on the side of the Americans.

One verse of a popular mid-sixties song in Neapolitan dialect was:

Tu vuo' fa' l'americano
mericano, mericano...
ma si' nato in Italy
sient a mme: nun ce sta niente 'a fa'
ok, napulitan!
tu vuo' fa ll'american
tu vuo' fa ll'american

(You want to be American
merican, merican
but you were born in Italy!
listen to me, there's nothing to do
Okay, Neapolitan!
you want to be American
you want to be American)

The song spoke of rock n' roll, whiskey and soda, and baseball. Because of its catchy tune, I sang it around the house every day for an entire summer. Little did I know that the lyrics actually held a spark of truth from those times. The Platters, Elvis Presley, and Gene Pitney could be heard in every Neapolitan jukebox.

Via Col Vento (*Gone With the Wind*) was shown repeatedly on television, and there were long lines outside theaters when *West Side Story* opened in a few select Neapolitan theaters.

Jack "Limone" came to Capri to film a movie and the papers were full of his pictures.

Tonino from the courtyard chewed Brooklyn Bridge Gum with the image of the bridge on each wrapped piece. "How beautiful it looks," he would say. "I'm going to see it one day."

And when a Chevy Impala was parked in front of the American embassy, people stopped to stare at it in amazement.

Ah, America!

Most people in my grandmother's neighborhood spoke to me about America with admiration, but they also teased me about the eccentricities and pomposity of America's proud claims. At the tender age of twelve, I had the difficult and unwanted job of being the "American ambassador" to the Via Egiziaca and vicinity.

"Roberto, come here," urged Renaldo, the local baker. "I want to talk to you about New York. Is it true that the buildings are so tall that the tops are always in the clouds?"

I remember saying, "Yes" to impress Renaldo.

"And the cars are the size of three 600s?"

"Yes, very true."

"And the streets are so very wide that ours are a joke in comparison?"

"Yes, that's true too," I admitted, hoping not to offend.

"And I hear you also have Coca-Cola there?"

"Yes. That's American," I said confidently.

"It was invented in Naples," he corrected me, "and it was stolen and taken to America. And of course," Renaldo said, "you have the *krapfen* that we make here in Naples. That is very common in America, isn't it?"

"Well, no, we don't have that," I admitted.

"Such a big country and no *krapfen*? How can that be, Roberto? It's not possible."

I felt somewhat defeated, so I decided to tell him about baseball, pasteurized milk, and peanut butter.

"Butter from peanuts? That doesn't sound very good, Roberto."

And to finally put Renaldo in his place, because he was a baker, I told him that we had Mr. Chips chocolate chip cookies, which were way better than the Pavesini so popular in Italy. In return, he laughed and gave me a hot roll just out of the oven, the big, crusty 30 lire kind, and I took it, feeling a little foolish that I had been so earnest in my defense of America.

"Ciao to your Nonno," he said as I walked away, chewing away at the crusty little lumps at the top and the middle of the roll.

Some people had distant relatives who had moved to America many years before, and they harbored confused notions about life in America. The barber near the Pallonetto told me that a great aunt had moved to America and complained that people only ate cereal for breakfast and that the coffee was like poison.

"Why is the coffee so bad?" he asked me seriously.

I couldn't answer, since I didn't know anything about coffee.

"And why do people eat steaks every night?" I didn't know the answer to that one either.

"And is it true that there are no fresh vegetables, only frozen ones?"

"And what is better, Il Bronx or Brookolino?"

I told him that I thought the Bronx was a little better.

His aunt had lived in Brooklyn, he told me.

"Well, parts of Brooklyn are better than any parts of the Bronx," I replied diplomatically. This was becoming rather tricky.

"Maybe you know some of the family? Esposito, from Brookolino."

I didn't know anyone from Brooklyn, I told him.

"Why do Americans have such thin hair?" he asked.

"I have no idea," I answered honestly, but decided this might be worth looking into.

A taxi driver told me all about his family in "Newaaark, New Jerzzz." His uncle was a baker who introduced the superior Neapolitan method of baking to "New Jerzzz." Through his cousins he had also become a Yankee fan, the only one I ever met in Naples.

"Mel Stottlemyer, a grand pitcher, but not good enough," he said in halting English.

—ᴡ—

Pasquale had serious questions for me about America. He was very interested in what I learned in school, what the difference was between the two political parties in America, and how Americans regarded Italy.

I told him all the minute details about my life in the sixth grade, but I wasn't too sure about what Americans thought of Italy. The moment he asked me this question, I remember thinking how rarely anyone in New York asked me about Italy when I returned home after each summer. At most it might have been, "How was the weather?" or "Did you swim a lot?"

One thing that fascinated Pasquale was that America was composed of so many different kinds of people from varying countries and religions. He found this cosmopolitanism very appealing. "I think people there are not always in your business, like here. Even mothers-in-law, I understand, are not involved in your life so much there. È vero? Roberto, è vero?" (Is it true, Robert? Is it true?).

One day Pasquale called me over and asked me if I could crouch down, bending my knees, then sit my backside on the top of my feet and balance myself on the front part of my feet. I was used to doing this, so I happily offered him a demonstration. He approached very closely to inspect that I was doing exactly what he had asked.

"Yes. That's very good. Americans can do it. Italians can't. I saw American soldiers doing this during the war."

I told him that I sat like this very often. "It's really easy to do this, Pasquale," I assured him.

"Well, apparently it's not easy to do, because I know of no Italians who have done it. However, it's very convenient. Those soldiers knew what they were doing. After all, there is not always a chair available."

Pasquale always ended his conversations with a concluding thought. "After all is said and done, Roberto, most people are basically the same, American, Italian, or anyone else, whether they can sit a certain way or not."

—∞—

Neapolitans tended to compromise for the sake of harmony; I saw this trait demonstrated on a bus ride one day. It was a calm morning of sun and lazy clouds when my mother and I approached the bus in the Piazza Plebiscito. Ours was the first stop, and buses were lined up with doors open but without any drivers. The drivers would only get on the bus at the last moment, start it up, and take off. I could see a few people as I approached the No. 44 that would bring us to Via Petrarca and my Uncle Bruno's house.

When we got on the bus, a conversation was taking place between a man in his twenties and one much older. The younger man was speaking of how corrupt America was and how America was a threat to working people everywhere. The older man was defending America vehemently.

"Without America, where would we be? Would we be under fascism?"

"The Russians defeated fascism."

"I suppose you would like to live in Russia, then. Go live there, Napolitan, and then tell me how you like it. I'll wait for you."

"Do you know how America exploits us here? You have no idea."

"The young, the young," moaned the elderly man to the woman next to him. "They can bullshit all day but they know nothing. They know nothing of real history. They only know the crap they teach in the schools today, which is worthless."

Most of the other people on the bus merely seemed annoyed that their reading or their daydreams were disturbed—until the conversation became more heated.

"I'm going to come over there and teach you a lesson," said the older man, becoming more irate. "Let's see when I get through with you if they can fix you up in one of those fancy Moscow hospitals." He made a gesture to get out of his seat that startled everyone else on the bus, and I was starting to get very scared myself. Fortunately, he was bluffing and didn't budge from his seat.

Just then the bus driver hopped onto the bus along with the ticket collector. The driver closed the doors, sat down humming a song, and was about to leave when he noticed the argument at its apex, the combatants' loud screams flying back and forth. The bus driver looked impatient and said, "Well, are we going to go or what? Are we going to argue all day? I have a schedule."

The argument continued, however, and the other passengers were getting agitated. Finally an elderly man, inconspicuous during most of the conversation, stood up and shouted with authority, "È va be, fanno schifo tutte due. Andiamo." (Okay, both sides suck! Let's go.)

That did it. The yelling stopped and the two combatants looked out of the window, murmuring to themselves.

"But one sucks just a little more than the other," one man called out.

"Always, someone has to have the last word," I smiled to myself. Suddenly I thought, panicking, "Oh, no, now someone will start it up again!"

Fortunately, other than a few stares from his fellow passengers, nothing happened.

"What a day, what a day, what a day," said the bus driver. "Such agitation so early in the day. I'm already late for my first run."

It ended as so many heated encounters did, with antagonists settling their disputes in verbal compromise.

—ᴍ—

I was only eight years old in 1963 when President Kennedy came to Naples in early July. My grandmother couldn't walk well and would therefore not see him in his open limousine, but she urged my mother and me to go to the Piazza Plebiscito early that morning to find a good spot to see him when he passed by.

"Go down by Gambrinus. From there you might have a good view. How much I like him. I wish I could go too."

The newspapers and magazines had pictures of him, the

RAI television news had a segment about his life, and plates with an image of his face hung in store windows all along the Via Roma. Pictures of the president and first lady were being sold in the street along with small American and Italian flags.

My mother held my hand tightly as we made our way down the street and down the steps to the Piazza. We were an hour early for his appointed pass-by, but already the Piazza was filled. The pigeons had no place to land and twirled in circles above.

After staring at the back of gray jackets and elbows and legs for what seemed an eternity, a roar rose from the crowd and I climbed the base of a lamppost to get a clear view. It was him! He was tall and impressive, standing up in his car. Next to him was a much shorter man; this was Segni, my mother said, the president of Italy. The men waved and smiled, waved and smiled, while behind the car children were running and waving to the crowd as well. In a few minutes the crowd dispersed, but the excitement remained.

We walked back home and people congregated in small groups, talking about Kennedy. One woman was remarking what a bel' giovanotto (good-looking young man) he was.

I remember being happy that he was so much taller than Segni. I felt that I was a little taller that day too. When I got back to my grandmother's house, I told her all about it and how tall he was and she was excited that we had had a clear view of him. For the rest of the day, many of the people from the building were talking about Kennedy and asking me questions about how he looked and what he did. As a proud American, I was awash all day in the residual glow reflecting from him.

That night we were all eager for the "Carosello"—a show made up of intricate commercials—to end and for the RAI news to begin.

"Let's see, let's see how they show Kennedy and whether he had anything to say about Naples at the airport when he left," said Aunt Adele.

When the news came on, Kennedy was seen filmed from a camera behind the car. The little *scugnizzi* (ragamuffins) were between the back of the car and the camera, and most were looking back at the camera, laughing, jumping up and down, and making faces. Some were jumping on and off the car's fender. One yelled out to the camera, "Hey, Momma." I thought it looked like fun, but I saw that Aunt Adele was not pleased.

"How disgraceful! The president of the United States is in town and look at these kids. What are they doing? What will people think of us?"

My grandmother nodded in agreement and my grandfather just shook his head in wordless disapproval of the scene.

That night I was happy to be American, just like Kennedy. I wondered if, when he was in Italy, he ate Italian food like I did, or if someone brought him peanut butter and white bread so he wouldn't be homesick.

—∽—

In the mid-to-late 1960s, being an American became a little more complicated, and I often found myself in the uncomfortable position of defending American policy and culture.

Signor Doria was my Aunt Adele's boss. He was at one time the mayor of a small city near Naples and was also rumored to be a Communist, or at least very left leaning. When I visited my aunt at work, he would invite me into his large, intimidating office and give me a firm, steady handshake that made me feel very uncomfortable. On the wall behind his desk was a portrait of Abraham Lincoln. Signor Doria often reminded me how much he admired our sixteenth president.

"And how are you this year? I see that you have grown."

"I am very fine," I responded, knowing that more difficult questions were next.

"What is new in America?"

Besides finishing fifth grade, I could not think of other momentous news.

"Nothing. It's all the same as always."

"And your president, what does he say?"

I didn't know what he said. "He doesn't say much."

"He must have lots of things to say, your big President Johnson. He's the president of the most powerful country in the world and you are a citizen of the most powerful country in the world."

"He still doesn't say much," I insisted lamely, wondering how soon this grilling would end.

"He must mention Vietnam now and then."

"Yes, I guess he talks about that since we are in it."

"Yes, he must. And do you have any idea what he says about it?"

"No, not really." I had no desire to get entangled in a discussion of American foreign policy. Better to play dumb, I decided.

"And what do you say about it, Robertino?"

"I don't know a lot about it."

"That is because you are so smart. Best to stay out of the whole mess of politics," he pronounced. "Good boy, put it here," he indicated, sticking out his hand.

Gratefully, I smiled and shook his hand, tacitly agreeing that today's interrogation was officially at a close.

—⚬—

Signor Doria wasn't the only person who brought up Vietnam. Giuseppino, who teased me about there being no cheese in America, asked me lots of questions about Vietnam. He wanted to know if I had any special insight into why the United States was there. He told me he didn't understand it at all. The baker and the barber asked me about it too.

Pasquale wasn't satisfied with leaving things unresolved. One evening we were eating tomato sandwiches and *panzarotti* (fried dough balls) under a full moon of white and silver light. Pasquale was trying to tell me what the Cold War was all about; he would begin a phrase, then hesitate and start all over again.

"It's like two bullies..."

"America and Russia are like two brothers..."

Just then his wife, Titina, walked by. "Leave Robertino alone. He doesn't want to talk about such things. Let him eat in peace."

"Okay, okay," said Pasquale. "Both countries are waiting for the other one to make a move, but neither one has the courage to make a move. They're both scared. And little Italy is the middle. Well, let's hope neither makes a move. That's all. Eat the tomato sandwich, Robertino. America won't win in Vietnam. But it won't matter. No one will make a big move. So things will just continue as they are. But one thing is sure. You won't get a headache tonight if you eat those tomatoes. It's almost impossible to get a headache if you eat tomatoes."

My grandmother and my Uncle Bruno were also opposed to the war. "America will go bankrupt with a war now," said my grandmother. My uncle agreed, adding, "There is no way to win."

I never heard my grandfather comment on Vietnam. What he really hated was the United Nations. "Bunch of *farabutti* [crooks]," he said every time Secretary General U Thant appeared on the television screen.

Others argued passionately about the Cold War. The words,

"America" and "Russia" whirled about in many Neapolitan conversations in the mid-1960s. I could not understand any details of these conversations but did catch the general feeling of the combatants. I remember a picture of Johnson and Brezhnev on the cover of *Epoca* magazine with a headline that read, "*I Nonni Della Pace*" (The Grandfathers of Peace).

"Grandmother," I asked her one day, "Why does it matter that both men are grandfathers?"

She laughed, saying that I had not understood the metaphorical intent of the headline. "They are like grandfathers of the whole world, just like yours is Nonno," she explained.

Most people sided with America. But most peculiar was the way political arguments ended amicably—with a "summing up" acceptable to both sides. The ardor of political discourse was no more heated than had it been about the merits of the Ferrari versus the Lamborghini, or whether Florence or Venice was the more beautiful city.

—ɯ—

Perhaps in America we had been conditioned to the unavoidable march of progress. We had followed the Mercury, Gemini, and Apollo astronauts on their missions into space, around the earth, and to the moon, so landing on the moon was the next logical step.

I was in Naples in the summer of 1969. For Neapolitans, there was a great range of opinions about the moon landing: men on the moon seemed impossible, not desirable, and the concept was barely believable.

Maria, my grandmother's housekeeper, said it couldn't be. The natural order of life would be upset.

Giuseppino asked me if I really believed it. "It is some kind of a trick," he said.

Pasquale thought that little good would come of it in the

long run. He said there were too many problems right here on the earth.

Uncle Bruno thought it was a turning point in history.

But whatever they believed, as the "Americano" in their midst, I was the recipient of everyone's enthusiastic judgments.

There were only two television stations at that time, the RAI 1 and the RAI 2. All the way down the *vicoletti* (little streets) on most evenings the same programs blared out from open windows and doorways, so one could take an evening walk and still hear the news or the latest show. In mid-July that summer, televisions were a little louder and the chatter around the dinner tables seemed a little softer. The radio news or television coverage of the moon landing continued several times a day as commentators checked on the progress of the mission. Yes, the launch had gone smoothly, to the relief of listeners worldwide. The voyage was proceeding normally and all the docking maneuvers went as planned.

It always gave me a small thrill to hear Mission Control describe in English what was happening, just before the louder voice of the translator overlapped it and the voices from Houston faded into the background. These voices from America were confident and competent. Every day of the mission affirmed how complex a mission it was and how capable Americans were who handled it. In this contest between Russian and American technology, America had won!

I was congratulated as if I deserved some of the credit. "Well, thank God you did it, Roberto. I'm glad the Russians didn't do it first," the baker told me. He took a few hot rolls from a bin and wrapped them very carefully as if to make them seem more precious, then presented them to me. Placing them in a bag, he held the bag up to admire it and placed it gently in my hands. "These are for you and for Il Signor Armstrong. Give him one of these."

The night before the landing, I was eating in a small restaurant with my family. When the waiter learned that I was American, he would call me "Little Mr. Armstrong" every time he brought me something.

"Here is bread for little Mr. Armstrong," he would announce, "and here is water for little Mr. Armstrong."

When we left, he called out, "Have a good walk on the moon!"

I saw Mr. Doria a few days before the moon landing. Unlike others who had confided their thoughts to me, he was more circumspect. He felt that the moon landing would certainly be an achievement for mankind, but that it was not particularly an American achievement—emphasizing the word "particularly." In fact, he pointed out that many great scientists from all over the world had made the moon landing possible. I remember his telling me that Werner Von Braun was German and that he had designed the rockets that made the voyage possible.

"This will be a great moment in history—for all mankind," he affirmed. Then he shook my hand with such firmness and authority that it made his words resonate loudly. I had an inkling of what he was saying, although I wasn't sure if he was trying to make me feel bad about being American. Over the next few days, however, I was to hear this sentiment many times. This was an important day for mankind—not just for America.

Despite what anyone said, I was very proud of our having won this contest—much like having won a baseball game. My team was the winner, and Neil Armstrong was our winning pitcher.

Uncle Bruno was the most excited about the moon landing. He read the papers incessantly in the days leading up to the walk, and he explained all the technical problems that had to be overcome. With glasses, spoons, and forks representing the rocket, the landing craft, and the astronauts, he demonstrated how everything should work. He told me what a great achievement this would be for all mankind and what a turning point in history this would be.

On the night of the walk, the streets were bare of people, but voices of commentators on television boomed in the street. We were dining out that night, and for the first time in my experience I saw that we were the only patrons in the restaurant. Uncle Bruno could not stop talking about what was going to happen. He told the waiter that he had "an appointment with the moon," but the waiter merely shrugged as if to say, "Yes, yes, I know all about it. So what?"

We walked home accompanied by the voices of Mission Control and the Italian translator. Later, when at last Armstrong's famous words were translated: "That's one small step for man...," a roar rumbled in the streets.

The next day all the talk was about the moon landing, how well the Americans had done, and how they could do anything, having shown how competent they could be. People who knew me offered their congratulations as I walked through the streets. "Congratulations on the moon walk. You did it," they told me, their voices reverent and respectful.

—∞—

By the 1970s, Naples was much less isolated than it had been. Everyone owned a car, travel to all parts of the world was common, and the icons of American life were everywhere. I could not have imagined the song "You Want to Be Americano?" having the cultural force it had ten years earlier.

I was still the "Americano" but was no longer exotic. Now I was asked questions about all the problematical aspects of

American life.

"Is it true that there are so many poor people practically starving in American cities? Is it true that blacks and whites hit each other in the middle of the street?" Now I was old enough to offer a thoughtful answer to these pressing concerns.

I was in Naples in 1974 when President Nixon resigned. People were perplexed that a scandal like Watergate could lead to the resignation of a president. After all, here in Italy political intrigue was a normal and accepted way of life. I was told that Americans were moralistic and naïve about so many things.

Over the years, American popular culture became more dominant while America itself became a less exotic place. On my last visit, *Seinfeld* and *Tutti Amano Raimondo* (Everybody Loves Raymond) blared from the windows while Dodger caps, Houston Rockets sweatpants, Timberland shoes, and T-shirts with both absurd and profane language on them hung in the windows of the fancy stores. I wanted to buy a T-shirt that read, "Seattle Supersonics Electrical Supply Company" before I found out it cost $40.

I thought of the song "You Want to Be Americano?" The world had become smaller and so many Neapolitans seemed not too different from many "Americani."

Chapter Five
—⟋⟍—
I Never Knew Gabriella Fabretti

I never knew Gabriella Fabretti, yet she is my mother. After I heard about my father's war experiences in Ischia, I learned a great deal more about his postwar life in Naples. He lived and worked for a year in Naples before getting married and moving to America. His story struck me with such force that I realized I had not thought much about what my mother's life was like before and during the war. Once I had learned a little bit about it, I wanted to know as much as I could.

My mother came to America from Naples in 1946 in an old tub of a boat with shared living quarters and seasickness her constant companion. Until this time, she had known nothing of a life away from her parents and her sister and brother. She had lived happily until the war, and then anxiously after it started, skirting danger and near death. But the family had all survived, and Naples, with its bombed-out buildings and impoverished population, nevertheless offered hope of a peaceful future.

To live in Italy would have been the natural course of life, but when my mother met a German Holocaust survivor, fell in love, and married, that course took a dramatic turn. My father wanted to move to America and leave behind the horrors he associated with Europe, and although she agreed, the trauma of the voyage to America was almost unbearable for her. She cried every day, convinced that she would never see her family again. America was too far away from Naples, and anyway, how could she ever afford to go back?

As a child, I saw her sadness at the dinner table, when she would spontaneously burst into tears. Was she thinking of her brother, her sister, her parents? Only years later would she mention the more benign aspects of her voyage. "I met a so-and-so on the boat, a famous doctor who lived on 86th Street." "The food was gourmet…we had potatoes every night."

Aunt Yolanda, my grandmother's youngest sister, was at the boat in New York to greet the new immigrants. She was an accomplished violinist who could no longer work at the San Carlo Opera House in Naples because she was Jewish, and she left Italy in 1940. She excitedly shared her great news—an apartment for rent had been found for the newlyweds!

Off they went in a new, black, 1946 Ford. My mother, now Gabriella Zweig, hadn't known how difficult it was to find a place to live in New York City, so it came as a surprise that finding living space should be an event for celebration.

My parents rarely spoke of the "little apartment" on 96th Street and Columbus Avenue, but I knew two things about it. First, it was pretty shabby and smelled of fish from the market downstairs. Second, however, this apartment remained a treasured memory, just as, when one grows older, youthful adversity later takes on the glow of heroic struggle.

Gabriella got a job in an Army Navy store; my father became a travel agent. My mother learned that as a travel agent's wife, she could go to Europe at a discounted price if she flew or took a ship there. Impossible, she thought, too good to be true. But it was true, and thus began the almost yearly trips to Italy. These early trips were also how, as a five-year-old, I came to hear about two places I would never have known about otherwise. One was Newfoundland, and the other, the Azores—two necessary stopovers at which to fuel up before arriving in Europe.

Years later my mother had become an American citizen and our small family was comfortably ensconced in our Bronx, one-bedroom apartment. It was now the early 1960s and I had been making yearly trips to Naples with my mother since my birth in 1955.

Traveling by plane gives one a sense of time. We know that we are two or three or ten hours away from our destination, and time aloft is measured by the discomfort of a seat. Ships, on the other hand, give one a sense of time measured in days and sense of distance. The vastness of the ocean is ever-present. Days are much the same, the ocean choppy one day, smooth another, but always featuring horizons never reached.

Each summer when we arrived in Naples, my grandparents would be awaiting our ship in their usual poses, leaning over the railing on the pier straining to find us on deck; they were as steady and constant as Vesuvius in the background. The sun shone down on our eager faces as our ship made its way to dock.

My mother would quickly fall under the spell of her family, adopting their rhythms and speaking only Italian. She would sit next to her mother, leaning in to tell her the little secrets of our life in New York.

All summer I lived in a purgatorial world, immersed in Naples yet with one eye on the life I had left in New York. My friends were playing on the boardwalk at the Jersey shore or playing baseball with their cousins in Maryland. I was imitating President Kennedy's voice for the amusement of Signor Doria and trying to convince the skeptical Peppino that baseball was just as great a sport as soccer. On Tuesdays I ran to newspaper kiosks to get the New York *Herald* to find out how miserably the Yankees had done. I would examine the box score closely. If they had been lucky enough to play the even more lowly Washington Senators, there was a good chance that they could sweep a double-header.

Amazingly, my mother's uneasy assimilation into American culture was now something left behind. No one cared here if she was a Yankee or Mets fan, if she liked Walter Cronkite or Howard K. Smith, or if she preferred Fords or GMs. However, she did buy me "English Corn Flakes" and the special "drinkable, pasteurized" Latte Berna milk from a special English store.

She did not ordinarily display much emotion, so I was always surprised to see her cry real tears at the end of each visit. I was too young to suspect that leaving might remind her of being torn away from her family in 1946, or that she may have had a premonition that the next summer there might be one less person in the family. Or perhaps she felt as if the long distance between them all would lessen their connection.

I, on the other hand, felt little sadness when it was time to leave. I was ready to return to my friends and to New York, my only true home.

But for my mother, return to the United States was a return to a comfortable yet unsettled state. She could still not embrace America fully or utter the simple words declaring her independence from her birthplace: "I am an American." Her family was too real in her life. I soon recognized that for her it was a betrayal to embrace a new country when her mother, father, brother, and sister were living so far away. To ease the separation, my grandfather wrote two letters a week, keeping us up to date about daily happenings, such as "Maria was sick this week," or "I did the food shopping," or "Ada is thinking of trading in her Fiat 600."

All went well until my grandmother died in 1967. Then the walls began to collapse on our summers.

—∞—

In some families the past is a subtle, yet tangible presence. It may not be spoken of at length or directly, but it emerges in whispers, hovering overhead like the vapors of a cloud. So it was in my family. My parents' Jewish experience in Europe before and through World War II was the "other member" of the family, the child hidden away who was best left alone and not spoken about to others.

Until I began preparing for my bar mitzvah in 1968, the last year of our annual summer trips to Naples, I had not thought about my Italian family as being particularly Jewish. They were my family first and Italians second; their "Jewish-ness" seemed incidental, as if it were an article of clothing that could be removed and then put back on.

My grandparents' house held little that was "Jewish." I don't remember a menorah displayed anywhere, although there may have been one on a high shelf or hidden in a closet, along with a prayer book in Hebrew. Nor were there any Jewish holidays in the middle of the summer, so there was no reason to go to the synagogue or to light candles or to fast.

As is the case with many hidden things, however, when they are unearthed, they can unleash a torrent of discoveries.

—∞—

Despite the 1938 "Laws for the Defense of the Race" that were imposed on the Jewish community, the Fascist years before the war made up the benign part of the family's Jewish experience.

My great-great-grandfather, Giuseppe Recanati, moved his family from northern Italy to Naples in the late 1800s after a vacation during which he fell in love with the city. His daughter, Ida, my great-grandmother, moved there as well, along with his young granddaughters, Pia and Adele, both born in Torino.

My grandfather, Max, was born in Alsace-Lorraine, Germany, in 1884. As a young man he was employed at a bank and was sent to work in the Naples branch. There he met Pia and they began courting, spending many happy days together until he was called back to enlist in the German army at the outbreak of World War I. It was difficult for him to leave both Naples, where he had come to feel at home, and my grandmother, with whom he had fallen in love. Before he left, he vowed to return when the war was over and marry her.

Max kept his word. As soon as the war ended, he tried to go back to Naples but was delayed by missing paperwork. He finally got the proper documentation in 1919 and arrived in Naples in December, a time that later events would show to be fortuitous. Max and Pia were overjoyed to be reunited, and they married the following year.

My mother, Gabriella, was born in 1923, one year after Mussolini's takeover of Italy. The early days of fascism had little effect on Jewish life. There were very few signs of anti-Semitism among most people, and life for Jews proceeded as it did for most Italians. While our family was not particularly religious, they did attend synagogue on holidays.

Surprisingly, many Italian Jews were, in those days, ardent fascists, and they even made up a good proportion of the armed services. The only "Jewish" incident that stands out in my mother's memory in the first ten years of fascism was when someone asked her, "Do Jews really have horns?"

Between ages five and eight, Gabriella attended the Jewish Carlo Rothschild School. Carlo Rothschild was one of the sons of the patriarch of the Rothschild banking family and had established a branch of the bank in Naples in the 1860s. He donated the space for the school as well as for the synagogue, which survives to this day.

Once a month Gabriella frequented a Jewish social club for children sponsored by the "Association for Jewish Women of Italy." Here she met other Jewish children and celebrated holidays; she even remembers receiving a Jewish newspaper for children.

Later, in public school, Gabriella joined a Young Fascist League, the "Piccole Italiane" (Little Italians). Her membership was actually a requirement for her to attend gym class, which she loved. Once a week a teacher came into the class to give "religious instruction," which, according to law, was not mandatory. My mother, along with a German Protestant girl, would excuse herself and go into another room. Her friends, who remained for their "religious education," thought my mother was lucky to be "getting out of it."

Gabriella would occasionally defend Mussolini to rebut my grandfather's anti-fascist diatribes. According to my grandmother, her husband, Nonno, had a "big mouth," frequently making fun of Mussolini and telling jokes about him to anyone who would listen.

"Please, please be quiet, especially in public," my grandmother would say, fearing that there might be consequences.

I still hear one of those jokes whenever watermelon is brought to the table. "Why is a watermelon like Italy? It is white, red, and green with a lot of annoying black things in it." The black things referred to the Black Shirts, the "thugs" who enforced Mussolini's orders.

—〰—

In May 1938 my Uncle Bruno was scheduled to have his bar mitzvah at the Naples synagogue. It was cancelled until the following week, because on that very day Mussolini was hosting Hitler with a parade in Naples. No one could guess that, after this parade, Italy and Germany would be bonded strongly together and the world would be moving precipitously toward war.

The following November the Italian government under Mussolini enacted "The Laws for the Defense of the Race." Among other statutes, it forbade "mixed" marriages between Jews and Italians; forbade Jews from holding many jobs, including with the government; forbade Jews from having non-Jewish maids and housekeepers; and forbade Jewish students, teachers, and professors from studying and working in schools and colleges. Some people were truly upset about the edicts while others thought them proper. Most were indifferent.

My Aunt Yolanda, a violinist at the San Carlo Opera House, lost her job, as did her sister, Adele, who worked in a store. Yolanda moved to America and eventually played in the Pittsburgh Philharmonic under the direction of Bruno Walter.

When my great-grandmother informed Silvana, her housecleaner, that she could no longer work for the family, the woman, a loyal and trusted friend of the family, asked, "Why not?" My grandmother explained that the new laws forbade it, but spunky Silvana replied, "I don't care. I'm still going to work for you." And so she did.

In July 1938 my mother finished tenth grade but could not continue her studies in the high school she had been attending. Since there were now Jewish teachers out of work and Jewish students were unable to attend schools, the Jewish community of Naples, numbering a few hundred, mobilized its resources to match up Jewish students with teachers. The Jewish teachers and professors were paid partly by the "community" and partly by the students' parents. My Aunt Lietta was very active in organizing this movement, even letting her home be used as a makeshift classroom.

The law stated that if there were at least ten attending students, a "Jewish" school could be established, something that was possible only at the elementary level because there were too few Jewish children in the upper grades. My mother, however, traveled around town with three other students to study with the Jewish teachers. The young, newly graduated Mrs. Isabella Coifman was a recent immigrant from Eastern Europe and taught general science and chemistry in her house. The elderly Professor Del Valle taught Italian literature, Latin, and Greek in her house as well. The white-haired Professor Susani did not want anyone in his house; he taught mathematics to the four Jewish students in one of their houses.

One of the Jewish teachers, Renato Del Monte, emigrated to America that year, and a gentile friend of his, took over the philosophy class. Professor Graziani was a renowned economist. Ironically, Mussolini would often quote from his economic theories. Since he was not at the university anymore, he taught whomever he could, and Gabriella was lucky to have him teach her tenth-grade economics.

Former friends were now seen less often, although they did get together and greet each other in public. My mother knew that one girlfriend's father was a "biggie in the Fascist party," so she avoided her, fearing that a meeting would cause problems for both of them. One day her friend approached and asked, "How come you don't say hello to me anymore?" My mother told her that she thought her friend's father would not want them to be friends anymore. "Don't be silly," her friend replied, and they saw each other often after that.

The only person who avoided my mother was her German teacher, who had previously been Jewish but converted when she married. She walked right by the members of my mother's family as if they were strangers.

In order to pass from one grade to another, students had to pass the "official" final exams, which even Jewish students could take with the rest of the graduating class. In June 1940 my mother sat down to take her exams in the public school. However, just as she was about to begin her first test, the principal walked in and recognized the former student of his school. He called out, "Gabriella, go to the back of the class. You may not sit with the others." This came as a great shock to her and left a deep wound. It was the first time that Gabriella had been singled out in such a personal manner.

At the beginning of the 1939–1940 school year one of the teachers suggested that the few Jewish students in his class might condense two years of study into one, and so it was decided to do so. Unlike in the American system, thirteen years of classes were required for the baccalaureate or high school degree.

In June 1940 at the same time that Italy entered into the war, Gabriella took her final exams for the high school degree. One could write an essay on a literary or political theme. Most students chose the political, a way, they thought, of ingratiating themselves with the teachers. Their essays consisted mostly of extolling the virtues of Mussolini and fascist government. But my mother chose the literary theme.

"Finally," one satisfied teacher told Gabriella after grading it. "I was getting tired of reading the same message again and again!"

During this time my mother acquired a young suitor, a boy who liked her very much, my mother recalls fondly. One day he approached her mother with a very important question. "In theory, would you mind if a gentile boy were to marry your daughter?" Her response was, "The matter is not up to me. It's up to Il Duce."

Because my grandfather was classified as a "non-Italian Jew," having arrived in Italy in December 1919, he was ordered to leave Naples, now a "war zone." The family moved to Florence in the first of many moves to many different cities. Soon the full effects of war were upon the family

—⚒—

Being separated from her friends and having to go to school apart from others was humiliating, but during the war such decisions could be a matter of life and death. Even giving a soldier the wrong answer or walking down one street instead of another could lead to immediate death or deportation to a concentration camp.

For everyone who lived through those chaotic times, four dramatic days would later stand out as pivotal:

JUNE 10, 1940:

Italy declared war on the Allies.

As Nazi panzer divisions crushed French forces, Mussolini was eager to take part in whatever spoils he could win from a defeated enemy. Perhaps afraid that peace would arrive before he could gain any benefit from defeated France, Mussolini wished to declare war days earlier but was held back by Hitler, who wanted to see the enemy totally vanquished first.

On June 10, before a cheering crowd of over 200,000 people in front of his office in Palazzo Venezia, Mussolini declared that "the hour of irrevocable decisions" had arrived. The declaration of war was handed over to the ambassadors of Great Britain and France.

I remember hearing a recording of this speech when I was a small boy. I was scared, yet fascinated by the man's determined voice and the approving crowd. Theatricality and bombast were mixed in fearful collaboration.

At that time my mother was studying for her high school final exams in Naples. A few days after the declaration two Italian soldiers appeared at the house demanding to be admitted. They were there to take my grandparents to prison under fascist law, leaving my mother, age seventeen, her brother Bruno, age fifteen, and her sister Ada, age thirteen, alone.

My grandfather, Max, a German Jew, had arrived in Italy in December 1919 but had never become an Italian citizen. Had he arrived in 1920 or later, he would already have been expelled, but as it was he was still subject to imprisonment as a foreigner, despite having an Italian wife and three Italian children.

Trembling and beside himself with worry, my Uncle Bruno ran to the home of my great-grandmother, Ida, and great-aunt, Adele, and told them what had happened. Adele agreed to accompany him to the police station, arriving only in time to see Bruno's father being shipped off somewhere in a truck.

Bruno ran after the truck in tears, calling out to his father, "Where are they taking you? Where are you going?" But there was no answer. The truck sped away, leaving Bruno trembling with anxiety. Meanwhile his mother, Pia, was taken to La Questura, a police station. Bruno ran home, slammed the door, and screamed out to the family, "Hanno preso Papa!" (They have taken Dad!). Shocked, the family now had to decide what to do next.

My mother later went to the jail with her aunt to try to see her father but learned that special visitation papers were required from City Hall before the family could visit the prisoner. When the clerk asked why her father had been taken to jail, my mother responded that he had done nothing. "That's what they all say," he retorted in a bored voice.

That day my mother could not get the necessary papers to free her father, so she went to see an attorney friend of the family for help. While they were there, my grandmother showed up after being released from the police station, explaining that they had let her go since she was an Italian with three children.

My grandfather was finally released from prison two weeks later. He had spent the time with other German Jews in a cell, where they told each other jokes to pass the time. Despite the alarming developments of that time, my mother and her family resumed a fairly "normal" life, chalking up the terrifying events as an arbitrary enforcement of the law, common in Italy at that time, rather than to any foreboding of what was to come.

This temporary respite ended when the family learned that, because they lived in a "war zone" and because Max was not an Italian citizen according to fascist law, they would have to leave the city. They had a choice: They could live as "free internees" (nomads) or live in a camp. Although the word "camp" in Italy did not have the same terrifying resonance that it did in Germany, the family decided to move. Over the next three years, because of the law regarding internees, they were forced by the Italian authorities to move from Florence to Perugia to Rome.

SEPTEMBER 8, 1943:

*General Marshal Pietro Badoglio of the Italian army announced
Italy's surrender to Allied forces moving north toward Naples.*

The Allies' estimated arrival day in Naples was October 1.
Thus southern Italy was now out of the Axis and an ally of
the Americans, but northern Italy, including Rome, remained
part of the Axis and under German domination. My mother
learned from a high-ranking Italian general that, because of
the new situation, Italian troops all over the country were
putting down their arms and going home. However, Jews
were now in mortal danger from the Germans, who had suddenly become the enemy, since Italy was now on the side of
the Allies.

A friend of the family, a Yugoslav Jew, had a friend in the
Italian army. She brought him to my mother's family. He told
the family that the Germans were likely to occupy Perugia
and that Jews would therefore be in danger. Now my mother
and her family faced an important decision. My mother's
grandmother from Rome had been staying with the family in
Perugia, but staying there would likely be too dangerous, so
the family decided to take her back to Rome. Perhaps once
there, the family would be able to survive and someday might
be able to return to Naples.

Unfortunately, "internees" were not permitted to leave
Perugia, but my mother suddenly decided that the family
should go to the train station and leave for Rome immediately, despite it being "illegal" for them to travel. So, trying to
look inconspicuous, my mother and her family went to the
train station without luggage, seemingly on a pleasant walk.
When a train heading to Rome arrived, there was great confusion with excited soldiers going home, and there was no
one to take or sell tickets.

They managed to get onto the packed train. Confusion reigned. Soldiers from the north were stuffed into the cars, trying to get to their homes in Naples, southern Italy, and Sicily. Baggage hung out of the windows and everyone seemed to be talking about "The Surrender" and worrying about what would happen next.

My mother, her parents, brother, sister, and grandmother boarded the train along with the crowd. After several hours of standing in a crowded corridor, they arrived safely in Rome. The group immediately split up and went to stay with various relatives. At that time, there were no trains leaving for Naples, because the fighting south of Rome, especially near Monte Cassino, was too intense. Because my grandmother was too afraid to travel into dangerous territory, in a lifesaving decision the family chose to stay in Rome. My mother stayed with a cousin for the first two weeks, never leaving the house. She was afraid that her cousin would suffer repercussions for harboring an "unregistered" person. The cousin, in turn, feared that the concierge of the building, whose sympathies were unclear, might turn them in. The penalty for disobeying the edict was death. My mother later moved to stay with other cousins, Aldo and Amelia. In this neighborhood she was less afraid and ventured into the streets every day.

Other members of the family stayed with different relatives. Even though the Germans were occupying the city, the Jews were relatively safe until October 16, 1943, the historic day the Germans rounded up Jews for deportation to Auschwitz.

MARCH 23, 1944:

Although the Allies were trying to move north toward Rome, they were hampered by heavy resistance at Monte Cassino. It was the twenty-fifth anniversary of the Fascist party.

Italian fascist and Nazi dignitaries, wishing not to provoke the restless population, held some low-key celebrations in different parts of the city to commemorate the twenty-fifth anniversary of the fascist party. For some time partisans had engaged in various resistance activities, including bombing places frequented by Nazis. There was little reprisal for these actions, as the Nazis did not wish to advertise any partisan successes.

On this day, however, a major operation was planned. Every day, a column of German SS soldiers marched through Rome and up Via Rasella, a narrow street. The Italian partisans decided that, by placing a bomb in this street, they could inflict major damage on the Germans and raise the spirits of those opposing them. A plan was carefully calculated to inflict as much damage as possible. Forty pounds of dynamite were placed in a trash can on wheels, typical equipment for street sweepers. Via Rasella was a sloping street and the Germans always marched from the bottom to the top of the hill, so a lookout was placed at the bottom of the street. At the appointed time, he was to signal another partisan, Paolo, at the top to put the trash can in place in the middle of the road and light the fuse.

On this day the column of marching Nazis was late, but at about 4:00 p.m. they appeared and the signal was given to light the fuse. Paolo lit the fuse and ran toward the top of the street. The blast was enormous and could be heard in many parts of the city. A huge crater formed in the middle of the street and against a facing wall, and the street was decimated, with bodies lining the street.

Thirty-two Germans were dead, as well as a forty-eight-year-old Italian man and a young boy. The Germans apparently believed they had been attacked from the building, and they began shooting, killing innocent victims who had gone to their windows to see what was happening.

Almost immediately, people were dragged out of their apartments along Via Rasella and lined up with their hands in the air. They were rushed to the local police station for questioning; thankfully, most were eventually released.

After much debate about what kind of revenge to extract, orders came directly from Hitler: Ten Italians were to be killed for every lost German. Who would the victims be? The first targeted group would be Italian Jews who had been held in prison or were soon to be brought to Auschwitz, to be joined by other Italians who had received a death sentence. But still the numbers were insufficient, so the Germans gathered up other "criminals" beyond the established number. The "extras" would be killed as well.

On March 24, Gestapo police executed 335 Italians in a cave called the "Ardeatine Sand Pits," a mining pit dug out hundreds of years ago. The victims were shot at close range and stacked up on top of each other in one of the worst atrocities in Roman history.

At this time my mother was living in a convent, sheltered by nuns who knew she was a Jew. During the day she lived as a gentile; earlier she had decided that she would be known by the non-Jewish-sounding name of Gabriella Fabretti. Since she knew German, she was working as an interpreter for an Italian engineer who was collaborating with the Germans to build a defensive wall along central Italy.

On March 23, she had gone to work as usual. Her office was on a street adjacent to the top of Via Rasella, one building in. Part of her job was to give workers a pass, so if they were ever stopped by the Germans, they would be allowed to proceed. My mother secretly gave out some of these papers to friends and relatives and learned that on at least one occasion a relative was let go after being stopped by the Germans because he showed his "working papers."

On that March 23 my mother was leaving work at about

4:00 P.M. Just as she was about to open the door to leave the building, she heard a tremendous explosion from the bomb. Scared and shaking, for she knew something terrible had happened, she closed the door to the sounds of screams and shots ringing out.

What should she do? She was fearful of making the wrong decision, but something told her to stay where she was, and that night she slept fitfully in the office.

The next morning, still unaware of what had happened, she walked out of the building just in time to see a man who owned a print shop, along with his son, being taken from the first floor, put in a truck, and driven away. The men had been printing anti-Nazi leaflets, and she never saw them again.

It was moments like these when my mother truly believed that a benevolent "hand" had spared her. Whatever the source of this mercy, she certainly realized the arbitrariness of life and the way a small decision here and there could lead to life or death.

"Had I left a few minutes earlier from work, I might have been in the blast," my mother told me. "It was not my time."

JUNE 4, 1944:

It was two days before D-Day, and the U.S. Fifth Army finally arrived in Rome.

My mother was still living in the convent, awaiting the Allied "liberators." She remembers that it was a Sunday. Even though the penalty for listening to foreign radio stations was death, everyone seemed to be listening to Radio London. The station had been announcing that there was street-to-street fighting in Rome.

That afternoon my mother went to a concert. On the way home she saw dirty, tired German soldiers marching north. One kind Italian woman offered a German a glass of water saying, "Embe', pure loro so' figli e mamma." (Well, even they are sons of their mothers.)

The night before, soldiers were seen dragging along stolen cows or sheep to their barracks, but on this day cries of joy, not terror, could be heard. Despite the curfew, everyone was out in the street watching the American soldiers arrive, tossing chocolates and cigarettes to the populace.

From this day forward she was no longer "Gabriella Fabretti," but Gabriella Herrmann, her real name. She excitedly called her friend Nellie, who lived in the northern part of Rome. "Nellie," she cried into the phone, "the Americans are here!"

Nellie, a Jew, was also living as a gentile under an assumed name. Not recognizing my mother's voice, she said, "There is no Nellie here."

My mother said, "It's me, Gabriella, the Americans are here. Let's celebrate!" But for Nellie, the celebration would have to wait a few more hours. The Americans had not yet arrived, and the Germans were marching in long, slow columns out of the city.

My mother felt a flood of relief wash over her. Was it possible? Could the repression of the past five years actually be at an end? Would those who had occupied her country be punished for their misdeeds?

Yet, although she bore the scars of daily fear and intimidation, she had escaped relatively easily. Only later did she learn of the fate of other Jews who had been taken from her city to meet their deaths at Auschwitz. Only when she met my father months later did she hear the details of the horror of these camps and the tragic fate of millions. But on this day, for the first time in years, she remembers feeling pure happiness. Her family and the whole city celebrated for days.

—ɯ—

After the war, when Gabriella was living in New York, she would sometimes meet her tenth-grade philosophy teacher, Renato Del Monte, who was now also living in New York. It was the early 1950s, and together they organized a yearly reunion of Neapolitan Jews in Greenwich Village. Despite people warning my mother not to be seen with the "communist professor," she continued to attend the meetings for many years.

The Jews who had remained in Naples survived. By the time the Nazis briefly occupied the city, they were losing the war badly and never did round up Jews as they had done elsewhere. However, some refugees who had moved to other cities in Italy or were deported to their countries of origin were captured and died in concentration camps.

—ɯ—

Every time I arrive in Naples, its sights, its people, and its sounds resonate. Because of my mother's experience, history runs down its streets and echoes at me from its walls.

The Jewish population of prewar Naples was probably about 600; in the Naples I knew during the 1960s and early 1970s there were probably fewer than 200. Yet, despite these diminutive numbers, the roots of Neapolitan Judaism were deep and its history intricate. As a young boy I was surprised to see Jewish symbols carved in tombs in Pompeii. Some Jews in Roman times had arrived in the Naples area as free traders, while others were brought as slaves to work for wealthy families. Subsequently, Jews had been left alone to follow their lives in relative freedom until the 1500s during the Inquisition. At that time, when Naples was under Spanish domination, they were expelled from the city.

I never have come to a firm conclusion about the role that fascism played in relation to Italian Jewish life. My mother does not speak in ominous tones when she thinks of her prewar experiences. Her anecdotes about being separated from the gentile population are related in muted tones and even with humor. Yet despite the years since her girlhood, she cannot shed those feelings of humiliation when she was forbidden to attend school with her friends.

I remember my Uncle Bruno arguing about Mussolini with a friend of his. He took offense to any suggestion that Mussolini should be compared with Hitler. I recall him saying, "In an interview with Emil Ludwig [a German journalist] in the early 1930s, Mussolini stated that the Germans use the Jews as scapegoats." Yet, as a sign of his ambivalence, Bruno seemed equally agitated when his friend downplayed the damage that Mussolini had done to the Jews in Italy. "He was evil and anti-Semitic," Bruno screamed as a final judgment.

In the late 1960s I would sometimes see swastikas in Naples painted on the sides of buildings. They shocked me, but Neapolitans seemed to accept these as part of the landscape. I once spoke to a woman who had been my age, twelve, when the war started. "Why wasn't anyone offended by the swastikas?" I wanted to know. "And why didn't people wash them off the walls. Were they offensive only to Jews?"

"Oh," she said offhandedly, "the people who drew them are just some loony nuts. There are always a few people like that around, but they're harmless."

Upon hearing that, I felt deflated because my righteous anger had not struck a chord. At the same time, I was offended that a symbol as offensive as a swastika could be dismissed so simply. Yet I also remember feeling, despite my indignation, that this woman had lived through the horrors of war whereas I had only heard about them.

In 1990 I was in Naples during Yom Kippur. I went to the synagogue with my mother and father to attend services where I had had my bar mitzvah many years before. However, this time military men were standing guard over the entrance with machine guns. There were rumors that a terrorist attack aimed at Jews might be taking place.

"What a crazy world we live in," my mother said. I immediately wondered if these uniformed armed men guarding a synagogue brought back unhappy memories of the war for her. But when I looked in her eyes for any signs of sadness, I saw none. Instead, she was eagerly looking at an old acquaintance she wanted to greet.

"Yes, it is a crazy world we live in," I thought at that moment, "but it's the only world we have."

And for Gabriella Fabretti, who learned as a girl how precious life is, it is a world that offers a new opportunity for her loved ones every single day.

Chapter Six

—∽—

Maria

I told Maria that soon people would be walking on the moon. As a well-informed twelve-year-old American boy, I knew what I was talking about. Astronauts were walking in space and had been preparing for the big event for years. I had seen the astronauts going into space on television with my own eyes.

"It's impossible," she countered. "The moon is sacred and God doesn't wish for it to be disturbed. Even if it was shown on television a million times, I would not believe it," she continued firmly. "The Americans are good at faking those things. God would not want it—he would most definitely not want it. The moon is for looking at, and for kissing in its light when you are with your boyfriend or girlfriend, but it is not for walking on."

Maria, in her fifties, was my grandmother's housekeeper; like Pasquale, she was one of the people who came into the orbit of my life in Naples every summer. (Most housekeepers were named Maria, except for a few who were named Anna.) Her arrival was announced early every morning by her clumping flip-flops, her high-pitched voice, and her numerous large bags and pocketbooks filled with aprons and kitchen implements that she needed for her work.

Every morning she brought along groceries for the day's meals and placed them where they belonged while singing a Neapolitan song. Later she would sit with my grandmother and go over the bill for all the food items. "The fruit is going up every day, Signora, just like everything else," I remember her saying many times. In return, my grandmother would give her the "skeptical eye," the kind of look that could make you feel as if she had just caught you in an indecent act—or worse. However, Maria would proceed to put on her apron and get busy, more or less cleaning up, dusting where there was no dust, and sweeping where there was nothing to sweep. A cherry found under the dining room table one December did nothing to boost her reputation as a meticulous housecleaner. After walking around with her feathery duster, she would settle down at the table to cut green beans and peel potatoes, readying all the accoutrements for the impending meal.

Maria was short, on the hefty side, and had a crooked eye, so I was never sure if she was looking at me or at a table that needed dusting. I couldn't tell from the subject of her conversation either for she held continuous chats with herself and imaginary listeners.

She lived, sometimes, with a husband who was, according to her, an unemployed, philandering dipshit bum of a man who disappeared for days at a time. Her meager salary had to support him and a daughter who was an extravagant-spending, would-be movie star. Part of her daughter's eccentricity was her desire to leave the block she had grown up on and take a bus to a different part of the city. She would also occasionally buy a dress and want new shoes. I don't remember ever seeing her, but for some reason I imagined her to be good-looking. On the other hand, Maria's husband looked like Popeye with a hangover. Her tirades, directed at no one in particular, were usually about him. When my grandmother asked her once who she was talking to, she said, "To the general public."

Maria feared just about everything. She never left the street of her birth, which fortunately was the same block my grandmother lived on. She was afraid of traffic in the busy part of town and the crowds, noise, strange people, and strange stores. She seemed incredulous that I would take a walk and wander into town as if it were nothing.

Maria was also afraid of roaches, bees, spiders, flies, and dust balls dancing in the air. Her resulting scream when coming across one of the above sounded as if someone was being stabbed to death. Who would have guessed it was Maria reacting to a fly taking off after she had put her coffee mug down on the table? One day she screamed so loudly that I thought she had found a corpse in the bathroom. A cockroach had scurried into a crack in the floor when she entered the room. She was frozen, her eyes glued to the spot where the roach had been.

On another occasion she opened the door to a room where I was exiting. As she opened the door, I found myself staring at her contorted face. Her mouth remained open and the shriek, which I thought could be heard halfway to Rome, vibrated and rattled in my head. She might have been the model for Munch's "The Scream." For days afterward, I could hear a slight whistle in my ears—fallout from her scream.

Maria's worldview did not include any scientific accomplishments after the birth of Galileo. She did not ascribe to the concept of a Copernican universe; for Maria, the earth was at the center of the universe, as any child could rightly surmise. The sun and all the planets and stars moved around the earth. Radio and television were enigmas, and how they worked was best left unexplored. I remember my uncle telling her about radio waves that existed in the air. She listened politely, with the indulgent grace and feigned look of credulity one offers children who speak earnestly of their Martian friends.

I knew that Maria didn't know much about trains, because she once asked me why I had not taken the train from America, which to her was a faster and more comfortable mode of travel than a boat. She did know that America was far away. She asked me once if it was "after Milano."

Maria had seen pictures of an airplane, or "the flying gizmo," as she called it. She knew that people were going back and forth to destinations on them. However, she seemed rather skeptical about their utility.

"People weren't made to fly," she would say, as if settling the matter, at least to her own satisfaction. She did not wish to upset the world as she knew it.

Maria's theological views were greatly at odds with the major beliefs of the world's great religions. She believed that Jesus was Italian and Catholic and that he had lived in Rome in the Vatican sometime before World War II. Anyone could deduce that Jesus lived in Rome because that's where St. Peter's was, and as everyone knows, St. Peter's is Jesus' home.

Maria believed that God had created a perfect world, with the earth at the center of the cosmos and Italy at the center of the world—a world that was obviously flat. God was everywhere, she would always say, something that I was very unsure about myself.

One day Maria caught me staring into the toilet bowl. "I am looking for God," I told her as she ran out, praying for my soul. Another time I looked for God in the freezer behind the frozen ices, only to receive a terrible electric shock that left a black, singed scar on my hand. Maria was sorry about my scar but seemed smugly satisfied that she had triumphed over my doubt. God spoke by sending messages meteorologically; storms reflected an angry God just as good weather reflected a happy one. Natural disasters were the surest signs of "His" displeasure, followed closely by car accidents. Driving a car was an unnatural act.

Maria's favorite word was Gesù (jezoo). Most sentences, regardless of content, were preceded by this word. "Gesù, it's hot in here. Gesù, did you see that? Gesù, what are you doing?" For more extraordinary events, she would offer two Gesù's: "Gesù, Gesù, they killed a man on Via Roma." To signify shock, three Gesù's followed by nothing: Gesù, Gesù, Gesù.

If it was worth a foreigner's time to study English in order to read Shakespeare, or for an American to study Italian in order to read Dante, then it was worth studying Neapolitan in order to listen to Maria. She spoke it truly, with the color, emphasis and nuance that created a language of special music.

Then one summer Maria was not at my grandmother's house. She had retired because of ill health. Her absence left a void in my life and reminded me of the richness of everyday life that I had almost always taken for granted. Maria's views had astounded me, and her comfort in her own ignorance perplexed me. But when she was gone, how much duller and less colorful the little world that made up my grandmother's house seemed.

Chapter Seven

Peeling Grapes and Other Mealtime Rituals

Meals at my grandmother's house were not just meals—they were events. After I arrived for the summer, I soon learned that there were rules for anyone who wanted to sit at her table. Everyone had to appear for each meal at the appropriate time—this point was nonnegotiable. If I missed a mealtime by a few minutes, such as the 1:00 P.M. lunch deadline, I would be subject to somber recriminations and hushed, head-shaking murmurs from the grown-ups.

Back in the 1960s at my grandmother's table, breakfast was considered the only minor meal and could be gotten whenever I happened to wake up. A cup of espresso with boiled milk and a slice of off-handedly toasted bread or a krapfen donut or a brioche was sufficient. If I asked for cold cereal such as corn flakes, the reigning favorite back home in those days, I was told this was a breakfast only for Americans or the English. My mother caved in occasionally and brought me to the English store on Via Chiaia to get "corn flakes Inglesi."

The unpasteurized milk that came in triangular cardboard

containers was deemed just fine, even though I had to skim off the cream from the top after it was boiled. This milk was called the latte centrale; for picky drinkers there was always the hard-to-find latte Berna, the American-style pasteurized type. Picky people were Anglo-Saxon types or Italians from the far north who had unfortunately adopted some of the characteristics of their Germanic neighbors. (The farther north one went, the "pickier" the people. Romans were insufferable because they were from the "capital." North of that, everyone was a snob. The areas bordering Austria and Germany were considered inhabited by a different species of human being.) Thus did prejudice reign, as it does today and probably will forever.

I enjoyed eating breakfast on the run. It was quick and efficient and, best of all, the only meal I was allowed to eat while standing. Americans, I was told, could eat standing, walking, or even running. In contrast, lunch and dinner required long periods of sitting still while we awaited the arrival of each course.

Lunch was actually the "heavy" meal, requiring a pasta dish along with a second course. The question was never, "Are we having pasta?" It was rather, "Which kind of pasta are we having today?" Vegetables and dessert were a must, the latter consisting almost exclusively, except on important occasions, of fresh fruit laid out in a bowl and served on a plate. Every year the quality and price of fruit was very different, and almost every year "last year's" was better. "This year the fruit isn't as tasty," I remember my grandmother always saying.

Even though all the fruit had to be peeled, it was mandatory to ask whether it had been cleaned yet. It always had been, but it was important that the question be asked. This was part of the ritual. I have a distinct memory of, at age five, peeling the skin off the grapes. My grandmother had insisted on it, since grape skin was "bad for the digestion." And besides, it had been sprayed with poison. So I remember working diligently to peel each grape, carefully placing the skins in a napkin. Peaches were also to be peeled, but since the poison used on them was not as strong, a good washing was considered an acceptable substitute. Nectarines need not be washed as vigorously, but apricots had to go through intensive scrubbing. Even nuts were washed, including peanuts.

Fruit, I was told, must be very ripe, never chilled when served. Many Neapolitans feared that fruit would eventually become tasteless and plasticlike if it was picked a month before it was ripe, as it was rumored to be in America.

Sometimes, early in the mornings, someone would yell out "frutta fresca" (fresh fruit), and if you screamed out the window that you wanted to have a look, up the stairs would come the farmer with his basket of freshly picked fruit. "They are all good, Signora," he would say, but my grandmother would inspect each specimen as if it were a diamond.

As far as the main course was concerned, it was understood that everything cooked should be swimming in olive oil. For food that was left on the plate, a piece of bread was available to "do the walk," to soak up the oil and remaining bits of food. After all, why waste good oil?

After the meal was over, it was time to sit quietly and read the paper, then fall asleep for a few hours. My aunt Adele could not read for more than a few minutes before falling asleep, so she developed the unique skill of holding the paper out in her two hands, in reading position, while she snoozed off for the afternoon.

Missing the afternoon sleep was cause for concern. After all, I was told, Americans had so many heart attacks because they didn't eat a good lunch and didn't nap in the afternoons. The English had some of the same problems. (The English were thought to be two-thirds American and one-third European. They also talked funny—through their noses—and, in the eyes of some, had started World War II.)

Dinner was, wisely, a light meal. Someone must have known that the stomach had to wind down before sleep, so cheese, vegetables, and fruit were sufficient. However, dinner could not be eaten before 8:00 P.M. If guests were expected, dinner was pushed to 9:00 P.M. or later. If the guests were from Rome, 10:00 P.M. was the appointed hour.

It was considered very bad form to remove the dinner plates before everyone was finished. I saw this custom demonstrated when my great-great-great-aunt, who I thought actually met Garibaldi shortly after the unification of Italy, had just finished eating her first piece of cheese when everyone had been finished ten minutes earlier. While the wait for her to catch up seemed eternal, it would have been reprehensible to have our plates collected before she was finished.

And of course the television had to be on throughout the meal. In the evenings the Carosello was playing, a show made up entirely of entertaining commercials. There was only one channel at that time. If you walked down the street when the Carosello was playing, you wouldn't miss a word of it—it blared out from every open window.

I was permitted two snacks between meals. Before lunch I could have a coffee or a lukewarm soft drink, and at 4:00 P.M. I could have ice cream or toast and marmalade. The latter was known as "marmalade time." The timing was important: Eating the afternoon snack before the appointed hour could cause gastrointestinal repercussions.

During my childhood days in Naples, I learned that there existed a list of mealtime abominations—foods considered merely bad to terrible. These included canned spaghetti and meatballs, peanut butter, bubble gum, ketchup, and white bread. TV dinners would be the worst, but since they were only for astronauts, they didn't really fit into the category of food. Chun King Chop Suey in a can was considered food fit only for Russian prisoners or stowaways on ships, but as a novelty could be tried once. We once brought a can for everyone in the building to taste. "What the hell is crawling around in here?" someone yelled out upon seeing it.

Eating out involved its own set of rules. Complaining was not permitted, and it was rare to send anything back, regardless of the severity of the problem. The exception was the one time I had a slice of cantaloupe that smelled like petroleum. The waiter tried to convince me for half an hour that his kitchen was immaculate and that his staff would vouch for that fact.

"How about if you just bring me another slice of melon?" I replied, hardly daring to hope. Desperate for support, I offered the offending cantaloupe to four others in our party. All agreed that the fruit did indeed taste like petroleum. After another ten minutes of discussion, during which a waiter tried to convince us that the taste was "in your head," I was finally brought another, more acceptable slice.

There were more "rules." Eggs in those days could be eaten raw, but milk had to be boiled, even though Italian cows were thin and "healthy" as opposed to American cows, which were fat and probably unhealthy.

Sodas for adults could be mildly chilled but had to be served to children at room temperature. A glass of cold soda frightened my grandmother, who insisted that the stomach could not take it and that severe cramps would follow the enthusiastic downing of cold drinks.

Many children, all foreigners, and mostly Scandinavians, were said to have died from stomach cramps after a cold soda. Coke barely fell into the category of a drink; it was closer to liquid poison. Cold Coke was an American invention, a plot to harm foreign children. When I pointed out that cold Coke was a favorite American drink, I was told that Gli Americani could drink them because their stomachs had developed a special immunity to the horrendous side effects they caused.

Other American anomalies included the ability to drink large amounts of watered-down coffee and to eat excessive amounts of meat. (An excessive amount of meat was more than four ounces per week.)

As to sandwiches, one must not have more than two slices of any given filler. The bread, it seemed, could be up to half a foot thick, but three slices of ham was not only wasteful and indulgent, it was unhealthy.

Drinking too quickly, regardless of the liquid's temperature, was also cause for alarm. Upon the first sign of cramping, one must seek immediate attention from a health professional or a grandmother. Coffee, wine, and beer in diluted form were not only good for children but as beneficial to infants as mother's milk.

In regard to feeding infants, it was obvious that mother's milk from any breasts, especially large ones, was considered excellent, but formula was wicked. If a woman's breast was too small to give milk, a busty maid must be found who could do the job for a small fee.

All vegetables, especially those with funny colors, were good, with the exception of carrots and corn. Carrots were for horses and corn was for pigs. Frozen vegetables, like cold drinks, were another horrific American invention, holding no nutritional value and barely digestible, regardless of how they were cooked. It was okay for astronauts to eat them, since fresh ones would go bad after a day or two, but upon returning to earth, they had to resume buying fresh ones.

Fish was considered an excellent food unless it was pulled from the bay of Naples, where fishermen had been hauling in their catch after exploding bombs underwater. Small fragments of the bomb might well be found in the whiting.

Tomatoes were known to be excellent for curing headaches and other neurological disorders, and at least one meal with pasta and tomato sauce was mandatory every day. Ketchup, despite its tomato content, should not even be mentioned in mixed company.

My grandmother considered the liver our most important organ, with most diseases caused by imbalances in its chemical makeup. If you were pale, tired, or in a foul mood, your liver was out of sorts. The cure was a brief vacation and eating lots of fruit.

The most delicate organ was, of course, the stomach. For this reason, we were to avoid cold food, which was especially damaging to the stomach lining and could even damage the pancreas. All foods should also be eaten slowly—eating quickly was an Anglo-Saxon invention introduced to Italians during the war. However, Americans and Germans were immune from the eating-too-quickly-and/or-eating-cold food-syndrome.

Away from the dinner table and on the beach, new rules applied. There was a brief and admittedly oversimplified way of deciding how long one had to wait before going into the water after eating or drinking different substances. My grandmother held a doctoral degree in "how-long-you-had-to-wait-to-swim-after-eating-any-food-item-or-combination-food-and-drink-combination."

"You had two bites of spaghetti with sauce. You must wait twenty minutes before you go in the water."

"You had three bites of a roll. Fifteen minutes."

"Two Perugina chocolates with nuts...seven minutes."

"A glass of cold water ten minutes ago and now a half slice of buffalo mozzarella...fourteen minutes."

An average full meal, consisting of a pasta dish, an entrée, vegetables, and dessert, required a two-hour wait before one could plunge into the water. The time must be adjusted upward or downward according to portion size and the addition or subtraction of any foods from the typical meal. Meat was particularly time-lengthening, since it took longer than any other food to move through the digestive system.

Chocolate bars required an eight-minute wait, peaches eleven minutes, nectarines ten, grapes one minute per four, figs six minutes each, and plums three to seven minutes, depending on type and size.

Wading in water up to knee level was permitted for adults who had recently eaten. (Adults were males over eighteen or females over twenty, unaccompanied by a mother. If a mother was present, females were still adults at twenty, but males had to be over forty if single. However, they were considered adults if married and over thirty. Two years could be subtracted for males for each child fathered.)

Waiting time for drinks was a complicated and constantly evolving science. As a primer for tourists, the following guidelines were helpful: Cold drinks required much more time than warm ones. Drinks with gas (fizz) also required more time. Cold, gaseous drinks were a lethal combination. To be on the safe side, a half hour wait after a cold drink was a minimum requirement. If you had two Cokes with plenty of ice, even early in the morning, you might as well pack up your beach accessories and go home.

Foreigners were often confused about the rules or just ignored them, much to their ultimate detriment. Swedes and Germans were particularly perplexed about proper waiting time procedures. As a result, their population was reportedly reduced after they downed cold drinks and took to the water without so much as a few minutes' wait.

In fact, several times a year one heard of a German or Swede who drank a cold orange soda or Coke, dove into the water, and was never seen again. "Another German died at

Riva Fiorita when he jumped into the water and never came up. He had a limonata with lots of ice just before he went in."

The Bay of Naples was reportedly filled with the corpses of unfortunate tourists from Munich and Stockholm. Should, one momentous day, all the Germans and Swedes who drowned in the bay after drinking cold sodas rise up from their watery graves, they would form an army of unfortunate souls—all of whom had ignored the rules of Italian grand-mothers.

My grandmother certainly had a lot of advice for me about all sorts of things. I took much of her advice to heart and was always surprised after returning to New York to see how little my friends knew about all of her rules.

In addition to the people who taught me so many things that I didn't know, public encounters always yielded memo-rable lessons, as the next chapter will illustrate.

Chapter Eight

Close Encounters of the Public Kind

On my walks through the streets of Naples, I never ceased being amazed at how Italians behaved so differently in public than they did in America. Nowhere could I find the requisite blank stare, the "safe" distance from others, and the modicum of efficiency usually seen in public institutions back home. People having to queue up in stores, markets, or banks refused to wait patiently. Instead they wormed their way to the front to peer boldly at the lucky holder of the number one position.

At first I was unprepared for this invasion of the little space I felt entitled to even in communal settings. But after a few encounters I was actually disappointed if events proceeded with the bland regularity that I was accustomed to back in the Bronx.

One morning I had to go to the Banco di Napoli with my mother to change some dollars into lire. On the bus, as usual, conversations were taking place every which way. It didn't seem to matter whether one was talking to the person in the next seat, the next aisle, or the front or back of the bus. And now and then a passenger who seemed not to be paying attention would suddenly stick his "two lire" in.

As I sat down next to a pudgy man in business attire, he called out to someone, "What does she want to do? Cut his balls off while he's sleeping, put them in a jar, and present them to him when he wakes up in the morning? And someone should tell the lady involved that the sausage is judged by its good taste and not by its size." I looked around, curious to see the other passengers' reaction, but no one on the bus seemed to give this comment a second thought. "Live and let live" seemed to be the order of the day on this bus, especially when it came to expressing one's opinion.

We got off near the bank, at the city center. A small but boisterous crowd was gathered outside the main doors. In a flash they reminded me of frenzied shoppers preparing for a race toward the "one-hour special" items at S. Klein on the Square, a huge store known as New York's "bargain central."

It was nine o'clock, and once the doors opened, everyone would surge forward to be first to enter the bank. "Madonna mia! Here we go," one woman announced when the doors opened. And the crowd, each one pushing to get an advantage, moved forward in a tightly wound ball of humanity.

We made our way to the information booth, where la signorina was yelling at someone who insisted he be called "Doctor." Apparently he didn't believe her when she said he must go on line 3, insisting she was putting him in the least advantageous position.

"If the gentleman does not trust my advice, he is welcome to go on any line he wishes," she called out derisively. He left the bank in a huff, muttering something about where he would like to send the young lady and her entire family.

When we finally arrived at the front of the line, my mother said she wished to change some dollars, and the teller presented a piece of paper to her. My mother was to fill out the forms and then proceed to line 1. The signore at that counter, who resembled Noah in middle age, looked over the form while my mother bit her lip anxiously. Then he pulled out a rubber stamp and started banging away in a flurry, back and forth between the pad and the stamp. After signing along a line wherever a stamped mark had been made, he gracefully fanned himself with the paper to dry the ink, and then placed the sheet neatly in front of us. His precise movements could have been those of an artist putting the final touches on his masterpiece.

Window number 5 was the last stop. After my mother produced the sheet and a passport, she was given the money. The 10,000 lire bills ($16) were as large as newspaper pages; as they were counted out by the teller, he was joined by the crowd swarming around us and peering around our shoulders. "Ten...twenty...thirty...forty," they shouted as each bill was laid out.

When we turned to leave, the space we vacated was immediately filled with new bodies as we walked out of the bank and into the bright sun.

Yet compared with a trip I made to the central post office a few days later, the bank folk seemed almost polite!

—∞—

The main post office building, just off Via Roma, was our destination.

Grandfather Nonno was already in combat mode as we walked up the steps. Having never been inside, I thought we were entering a great museum, but he knew better. Inside were dozens of windows, a labyrinth of hallways, and people determinedly scurrying about, as well as others looking around as if they were waiting to hear an important announcement.

Nonno had some vague idea about where to go first, although it seemed to me that navigating to the proper counter required the same instincts necessary to explore a Moroccan bazaar. There were no signs and no helpful directions, only chaos. In front of each window there were no lines, but rather clusters of angry people pushing, yelling, and complaining.

We joined a cluster where Nonno seemed confident that he was in the right place. Bypassing normal procedures, he yelled to the man in the window, "Is this where tax bills are stamped?" The man behind the counter was chewing on a large loaf of bread. He raised his arm high so it could be seen by all, and he pointed to a sign that read, "Lunch." It was 11:00 A.M.

A woman who was not part of the cluster in front of the window started yelling, "Madonna, Madonna, please let me get to the front. My baby is starving and will get sick if I don't get out of here."

"Then get her out of here and feed her. What are you doing here if your baby is starving?" a voice from the crowd called out.

"Just let her in, let her in," someone else retorted. The woman was in luck: the group stepped aside, and the woman walked straight to the front.

I was starting to think that this was exciting, that I was witnessing an unusual event, but then noticed the look of bemused indifference on everyone's face, including Nonno's. Arguments, interruptions, insults, and haphazard confrontations were common and taken in stride.

After a short interlude someone yelled, "Hey, Mister. How's about it? Is lunch over or do we have to wait for you to digest and take a nap?"

Amazingly, the man immediately took down the sign that read "lunch." When we got to the front, Nonno produced an envelope with money inside, but the postal employee said we needed to fill out a form, which we did on the spot. He then became a whirlwind of activity, his arms going every which way, stamping and signing the form much like the teller in the bank had done.

With that task complete, there was only one more window to visit. The form was now covered with stamped ink that stuck to Nonno's fingers. After turning in the form, we made our way to the exit, where I turned for a final look at the crowd. My last impression was of envelopes and packages waving in the air like flags at a war rally.

—∽—

In the summer of 1969 my Uncle Bruno took it upon himself to help my Aunt Lietta by collecting her tenants' rent. I tagged along, expecting this to be a fast, forgettable event.

We arrived at the front gate of the house my aunt was renting out, opened it, and walked out to the garden with Pasquale, the concierge, who was watering a plant with one hand and eating a piece of bread and tomato with the other. "They're waiting for you," Pasquale said. A small crowd had gathered in the courtyard in anticipation of my uncle's visit. "It's like this every month," Bruno muttered to me.

At first there was a general murmur from the whole swarm, but eventually the noise settled down and Antonietta, one of the tenants, darted forward from the crowd. She was wearing a black summer dress and yellow rubber flip-flops, which loudly flipped and flopped as she grabbed my uncle by the arm.

"Signor, Dotor, Ingeniere, it's good to see you. How is your family?" (My uncle had three titles because he was an engineer. A high school graduate got two titles, a fourth-grade graduate only one; however, on a business card, regardless of level of education, at least one extra title seemed to be acceptable.) "I know you are here for the rent, but there is one important matter I must speak to you about."

"What is that, Signora?" he asked, girding himself for the inevitable.

"You may not be able to tell by my outwardly youthful appearance, but I am a very, very, very, very sick woman. My liver has disintegrated so badly, the doctor can hardly find it. This has given me a terrible case of night arthritis, which comes when I must sleep and I can't. During the day I am so tired I can't work or do anything. Who is the little fellow with you? He is cute. I am very, very sick."

"I'm so sorry to hear that, Signora."

"Of course I know that the good engineer can do nothing about this. We know that you only collect the rent for the old signora, your aunt. But perhaps you could put in a word for me; she could lower the rent, even just for the rest of the year. Is this boy your nephew, the American? I am very, very sick, Signore. Oh, and I am Antonietta, Signore. Your aunt knows who I am."

"I will talk to her, of course. But you know there are always expenses that are going up. Your rent is two thousand ($3). That is very reasonable."

"Gesù, Gesù, in a year my liver will be the size of a peanut." She stepped back, to be replaced immediately by Alesandra and her twins, Tonetto and Pina. The twins were ten years old, always walked together step by step, and spoke almost at the same time. I had known them for years and used to think they were husband and wife. The only time I saw them separated was when Pina would say that she had to go home to start preparing dinner.

Alesandra made a small bow in front of my uncle. "The good dottore will indulge me for a brief second. What I have to say is so painful that my stomach is grinding away just thinking about it. It is no secret among all my good neighbors here, and if I am not mistaken, even to you, most distinguished Sir, that...that...my husband has abandoned me and the kids." She clasped her hands in a fist and held them up to her heart. "It is six months since he took up with the barmaid-whore from Rome and I have not heard from him since. We were a family of humble means before he left, but now we are really in a bad way...a bad way...a very bad way, Signore."

"I am sorry about your troubles. What may I do for you?" he asked politely.

"Oh nothing, we all understand that there is nothing you can do regardless of our troubles and afflictions and lack of means. We expect nothing, absolutely nothing. It is just that ...God forbid, your beautiful wife would leave you one day and you were so depressed you couldn't work, and paying the rent would be an impossibility...but thank God it is not so for you. You have a wonderful wife and beautiful children. Thank Jesus for that."

A very young woman with a limp now walked to us out of the crowd. " My father was wounded in Russia during the war. He hurt his leg. I have inherited a bad limp, most distinguished Doctor. Look at the way I am condemned to walk."

"The kitchen pipes are rusted, about to burst," a man burst out in an act of apparent support of the others.

"That is something we can look at," my uncle responded helpfully.

"Please come into our home for a cup of espresso and a drink for the boy," called out a woman who had previously been hidden in the crowd.

"All right," Uncle Bruno agreed, "but we can't stay long."

The small group dispersed as we followed the woman into her house. Her floors were black marble, her furniture ornate and heavy; my uncle sat down at a shiny rosewood table. The woman started to talk about taxes and possibly buying her apartment if, Jesus willing, her husband would be able to stay on his job.

I wandered over to a picture in a corner that held a small, lit candle in front of it, a kind of shrine. The picture was of Mussolini. An inscription under it read, "To our beloved Duce. May God preserve his precious soul forever."

The woman brought out a few cookies and some apricots. "Please, please eat for momma," she said to me. She then grabbed her heart with both hands and let out a long, exasperated sigh. "Ahhh, who knows how long the old ticker will keep on going. Please speak to the old signora for me."

"Yes, of course I will," my uncle promised.

I ate an apricot but didn't know what to do with the pit, so I put it in my pocket.

Finally we left. "Goodbye, most eminent engineer Doctor," she waved from the doorway. "Such a cute boy..."

We went out into the courtyard, where the twins were standing with their hands behind their backs leaning against a wall. A man peered out of one of the windows. "The pipes, the pipes," he shouted in farewell.

As we exited the courtyard, Pasquale was sitting in a chair. He nodded with a simple, knowing look. "I know what you've been through," it seemed to say.

My uncle was sweaty and agitated. "This was an easy one compared to last month," he muttered to me. But it didn't take long for him to recover from his ordeal. When Bruno and I had walked only a few steps out of that courtyard, his natural springy gait returned and within a few minutes he was himself, as if the rent collecting had been in the distant past. I too felt renewed—and found myself looking forward to the next time we had to collect the rent.

Chapter Nine

Aunt Lietta's House of Treasures

My grandparents' house, where we stayed for the summers, was owned by my great-aunt Lietta, who lived next door. Aunt Lietta was several years older than my grandmother and had married my mother's great-uncle Mario, a colorful entrepreneur who brought the first movie house to Naples. Uncle Mario also ran a movie studio in Naples that produced silent films. He passed away in 1936, long before my family and I had begun our visits in the mid-1950s. So for as long as I knew her, Aunt Lietta was a widow.

She came to be an important figure in my life, beginning when I was about five years old. No stranger to child psychology, she cleverly initiated a tasty ritual that I eagerly looked forward to. Whenever we met at her house, my Aunt Lietta would have a piece of chocolate for me. If anticipation is superior to consummation, each piece of chocolate was truly a treasure, for I had to wait a very long time between her offer of the anticipated gift and my actually receiving it.

First we would climb the many stairs to her little room. There she would take out a small stepladder. Up she would go until she was able to feel around inside her closet for that coveted bag of chocolates. It felt as if time stood still as she groped and poked. I stood below her, barely concealing my eagerness to receive today's treasured sweet. By the time she finally pulled the chocolate out of the bag and handed it down to me, I was salivating like a hungry puppy.

They were Peruginas, a coveted brand in Italy in those days, and were elegantly wrapped in various colors of cellophane. If the wrapping was gold, there was a good chance the little morsel would be milk chocolate, my favorite. If not, it was bittersweet, and I would have to wait another day before having a chance at my prized milk chocolate.

Because I had been trained to be polite, I didn't dare ask for another try at the milk chocolate, or for an alternate to the bittersweet chocolate. The ritualistic manner in which she retrieved each piece made it seem as if participating in this ritual was a special honor and that asking for another shot at the prize would be an act of supreme selfishness, a futile attempt to break a universal law of nature.

Oh, the innocence of youth! How her delicate little hand, stretched out to me with the golden-wrapped jewel, nearly brought me to tears of joy. "Let us see what we have here," she would say as I plucked the treasured candy from her hand.

Aunt Lietta's home might have been the setting of a Gothic novel. Although there were none, I could almost expect to find cobwebs between the folds of the thick, red curtains gracing the walls of her dining room. Along one side of the room stood two large Chinese vases. I wondered if Uncle Mario had actually gone to China to buy them.

The dining table had thick, ornate legs; lions' heads formed the feet. Hanging over the middle of the table was a chandelier that Louis XIV himself would have deemed "too rococo." Suspended from the middle of the chandelier was a small wire with a button to summon the maid from the kitchen.

Once a year my family was invited to Aunt Lietta's for the "Big Meal," a celebration for my family, just before we departed for our return journey to America. Reluctantly, I would dress up, wearing the requisite white shirt and long, dark pants. As the final part of my disguise, I assumed the somber demeanor of a young boy entering a holy shrine.

Invariably dinner would begin with a soup that was too hot. The meal would move from bad to worse—I didn't like the cannelloni, which appeared like clockwork every year. However, I became so engrossed in the solemn procession of food brought out on silver platters that I forgot to complain. Always polite, I would reveal only to my mother—and only through signals that others would not pick up—my unhappiness with the meal.

"Try not to cry this year when you see the cannelloni," my mother would say, already prepared for my covert signals of rejection.

On the plus side, I was compensated for the awful cannelloni by the rare opportunity to push the "call button" and summon the maid. I would pretend to order her to "Hurry up and take these dirty plates away," after I heard the faint ring of the bell from down the hall. I was so delighted by this rare act of power in Aunt Lietta's house that I would imagine that, once back in our Bronx apartment, I would hang a similar device from our kitchen light fixture.

At one end of the dining area were swinging doors that led to a small secret area, a kind of "reading room" that was off-limits to me. My attempts to peer inside were occasionally rewarded by a glimpse of the silk and velvet chairs and sets of leather-bound books. It wasn't until I was nine years old that I actually sneaked into the room with the excuse that I was looking for folding chairs I knew weren't there. As I turned slowly to have a look at the lugubrious drapes, heavy carpet, and robust, intricately carved furniture, I half-expected to find a skeleton nestled behind the thickly upholstered sofa.

Such was the otherworldly air of this cavernous room, similar to that found in the less popular wings of museums. I imagined these rooms when reading Gothic novels, and I suspected that Norma Desmond in *Sunset Boulevard* might have had a room like this.

In one corner I found an old encyclopedia titled Treccani, divided into several immense, dusty volumes. Reverently, I removed one volume and held it breathlessly, for it seemed to me that these books were precious and might have been handled by royalty. I was awed and intimidated by their weight and sheer massiveness. On the first page, a picture of the Roman Coliseum greeted me with donkeys standing in front of it. Other pages featured drawings of ancient Rome and busts of great men. I still remember my excitement as I became aware, for the first time, of the vastness of knowledge, the encyclopedic sweep of how many things I had yet to learn about the world. Beyond the covers of the books and beyond the bookcase was an infinite catalog of things, people, ideas, and places.

I recall having had a fantasy when I was very young that I assumed was shared by others. I yearned for a pill that would let me know everything, or at least enough to pass my next test. That fantasy dissolved the day I saw the Treccani encyclopedia. How could I give up the passionate struggle to learn about so many things simply for the joy of knowing them? From that day until I was much older, I loved peering into, holding, and walking around with big, fat books.

Now, after putting the reference book precisely where I had found it, I left the room so that its relics and ghosts would no longer be disturbed. On subsequent visits to Aunt Lietta's house, I burned with the desire to go into that room, but I didn't dare ask her for permission. She kept the door closed, never approaching it so as not to disturb the past.

In those days I had a friend named Maria Teresa, who lived on the bottom floor of my grandmother's house. Her father was a stern-looking *maresciallo*—an officer in the National Guard—whose wife always said he looked just like Gary Cooper. Whenever we met, I always had to prepare myself for his viselike handshake, which would leave my knuckles sore.

Maria Teresa was my age and pretty, but best of all she ignored the call of the afternoon siesta, that time of day when hardly a dog could be heard in the streets. A willing partner in crime, she joined me one afternoon as we sneaked into Aunt Lietta's house, hoping to find some hidden treasures in the little room. We climbed through a window and made our way past the kitchen, where we both stopped and stared in amazement.

My aunt's maid, a homely woman who resembled Margaret Hamilton in *The Wizard of Oz*, was sitting there, caressing a man on her lap. I recognized him as the handyman who took care of minor jobs in the apartments my Aunt Lietta owned. I was so stunned by this scene that for a moment I was actually at a loss for what to say or do.

What was I to make of this tawdry scene? Despite my confusion, however, the thought of my aunt sleeping upstairs while all of this went on "under her nose" set me on edge. It felt as if my aunt, slumbering in sweet innocence, was being betrayed. Then again, I didn't feel very good about myself, since I too had sneaked into her house. I rationalized these concerns by telling myself that I was simply an innocent trespasser while this handyman was practically having sex in my aunt's house. Did he think this was a brothel? Besides, I was family!

Maria Teresa, on the other hand, actually thought the whole thing amusing and suggested we go back the next day to see if they were still "doing it." Although I never saw a repeat of that startling tableau, many years later I heard whispered—the way adults whisper to each other when a child's present is hidden—that the "Wicked Witch of the West" had conspired with her lap-dancing partner to alter Aunt Lietta's will!

Most evenings Aunt Lietta would come to my grandmother's house and watch the Carosello with us, half an hour of commercials. These commercials were so good that they were actually the best thing on television.

Until I was about ten, there was only one channel. Then one summer everyone was excited to learn that another channel was airing for two hours every night. This extra channel was a source of pride for Italians, a sign that they were advancing quickly into the modern world.

My favorite commercials were for Brillantina Linetti, a gooey hair cream. I watched eagerly as a detective proceeded to solve a very complex case, of which we viewers were given a brief enactment. After being praised for his achievement, the detective would always say, as he bared his bald head, that he had not used Brillantina Linetti. Everyone would scream out in unison along with the detective "Non ho usato la Brillantina Linetti." (I did not use the Linetti hair cream.) Aunt Lietta once said of the veracity of the commercial, "Be, chi lo sa," meaning, "Well, who knows?" It was the only skeptical remark I ever heard her utter.

Oddly, even though she lived next door and only a bedroom wall divided her from my grandparents' bedroom, Aunt Lietta would have to leave her house, enter the courtyard, and climb the stairs in order to visit. One year, we were told that on our next visit we would witness a big surprise. On the ship on the way over, I could hardly imagine what it might be. On our arrival, we were escorted to my grandmother's bedroom, where we could see a new door. It led to my Aunt Lietta's house; now she could come and go as easily as if she were living in the same apartment.

Every summer Lietta would buy me a gift just before it was time for me to leave. She would ask what I wanted; usually I had no idea what I might want. Except once.

Brinkmann's was a jewelry store near the port that I would pass on my walks with my grandfather. Behind the clean windows, shiny watches were alluringly displayed. Could one of Brinkmann's watches be my gift from Aunt Lietta? Would it be too expensive? Could I let her know what I desired by suggesting, cajoling, hinting, or gesturing in the direction of chronometry?

I thought incessantly of the most practical approach to achieve my desired gift, even tossing and turning at night until I came up with what seemed like a long shot, but worth a try. On my next walk with my grandfather, I would stop at the window, stare at the gleaming wristwatches, and express my feelings of admiration. I hoped he would relate these sentiments to Aunt Lietta—if indeed he knew that she was thinking of a gift for me. I imagined that he would describe how strongly I had expressed my interest in these timepieces, at which point she would suggest that he purchase one for me.

Could this scheme possibly work? It would, of course, require a perfect alignment of various conditions. I knew that every afternoon Aunt Lietta would sit in the courtyard with the family. I hoped that this would be the scene of my hoped-for encounter between Aunt Lietta and my grandfather.

Days passed, and my aunt hadn't asked again about the gift. Our day of departure was fast approaching, but my grandfather was proceeding with his daily activities as if I hadn't even dropped a hint. His actions implied that, if I were to return home without a wristwatch from Brinkmann's, it would be of no consequence whatsoever.

The days were winding down, but the hours were infinitely divisible. How long the moments are, how they stretch and lengthen in tortured perpetuity, how indifferent is the march of time to our anticipated wants and desires. When the wheel that determines our fortunes spins and reaches the very lowest point, a reversal of fortune is in the making.

Conversely, how quickly and with what immediacy can a few simple words set the heart leaping, lifting the spirit from lethargy. When they came, the words were like a clear bell of victory, drowning out my fears of defeat.

One afternoon just before our departure, my aunt turned to my grandfather while sitting in the post-siesta loungers and said, "If you could take care of that little matter that we discussed on one of your walks, I would greatly appreciate it. The time is approaching quickly, whereby it would be too late then."

I immediately recognized the circuitous syntactical pattern employed in front of children, just as all children do when they are seemingly being excluded from information they are not meant to receive. To all adults, I offer the following advice: Stay away from this well-tested but desperate and ineffectual strategy. The very convolution of strained grammatical pattern and excessive verbiage alerts children to listen even more closely.

Listening keenly, I found her message vague, but promising. It had neither contradicted nor confirmed what I wanted to hear, and all I could do now was wait. The next morning my grandfather told me that it would be best if he went alone on his walk. He had "important business," and besides, wouldn't it be nice to sleep late?

I took this to be more than an omen; it was practically confirmation of a Brinkmann watch in the near future. With an ease and confidence that I rarely displayed in my entire eleven years, I walked around the house that morning, sipping caffe latte (an entire cup of latte, two spoons of caffe) and regarding the rooms with a cool indifference, as if I had just bought this little corner of the world as my domain.

As the day crept on, however, I began to experience again those nagging, dull misgivings. I surprised myself by my sudden lack of faith but couldn't stop asking myself whether picturing the watch on my wrist was premature. True, Aunt Lietta had given my grandfather a task, but was it "The Task"?

No, grandfather had not wanted me to go with him, which was surely a good sign, but perhaps my aunt had asked him to go to the bank for her. After all, she was the proprietress of a large number of apartments requiring business transactions. Because she hardly left the immediate neighborhood, it would not be surprising for her to ask him to transact simple business for her.

However, there had been, in the encoded message, a reference to time, and I was leaving very soon, very, very soon. If it were not now, it might not ever be, and I could end up with no gift at all, or perhaps with a shirt whose sleeves were too short.

That afternoon, at the usual gathering of relatives and loungers in the courtyard, I tried my best to hide my churning emotions, adopting an attitude of calculated composure. Halfway through the eating of ice cream, Aunt Lietta pulled out of her pocketbook a small, beautifully wrapped package and handed it to me.

For a second, I thought it might be a key chain, but upon unwrapping it, I found myself indeed staring at a gold-colored, 21-jewel, incabloc, Brinkmann wrist chronometer.

To capture my joy with mere words would be useless. Although the watch's second hand would fall off nearly twenty years later, I still feel a slight dash of mad joy when I catch a glimpse of it lying in my drawer. On the days when the batteries in my endless pageant of other watches ran out,

I would put on the "Brinkmann," strictly out of homage to Aunt Lietta and the miraculous, serendipitous procession of events that had led to my getting the watch of my dreams that summer.

If not for my Aunt Lietta, I might have regarded dignity of character as mere mannerism, the fashion "du jour" of her day. However, her elegant demeanor had a powerful effect on my understanding of how one's temperament can override the contrived postures of modern life.

When I last saw her, she was nearly 100, a diminutive figure lying in a bed, her body making a small impression along the four lines that were her legs and arms. At this stage, her body was little more than bones covered by flesh.

"Did you have a good trip from America?" she asked weakly, looking directly at me. I was shocked by her condition; this was a far cry from the Aunt Lietta who had offered me such prizes in my youth. I told her that I had had a good trip.

"Did you have a good trip from America?" she asked again. Then her eyes left mine and stared ahead, perhaps at Uncle Mario, who awaited her elsewhere, his photograph still in the place of honor on her bedside table.

Chapter Ten

World Cup in Naples

The train from Rome was pulling into the *Stazione Centrale* (main station) in early July 1966 when the man sitting next to me put his face to the window to peer outside.

"So this is Naples," he said. "It's so dirty! And look at the people milling around with nothing to do. Well, let's hope this stop is a short one."

I had heard him discussing his impending business trip to Sicily with the man on the other side of him. From his questions I knew he was worried about what he might expect when he arrived in Palermo, the last stop on the train.

"Will it be difficult to get a taxi at the station?"

"Can one walk around town at night?"

"Is it easy to find a telephone?"

I was only eleven years old and was returning to Naples with my mother, but even I had heard the stories about southern Italy, all told by "northerners." Supposedly, the south and everything wrong with it began in Naples and worked its way down. The people were supposedly lazy and could not be trusted. The only good thing I heard about the south was that the farther south one went, the cheaper the prices, even for the same brands.

"Buy the Tradate shoes in Naples," I was told once when in Genova. "They're ten percent cheaper. It's the tax we pay for living so far north. Everything costs more here. Did you notice, Roberto, that our 100-lire gelato is much smaller than in Napoli?"

Now, the man beside me kept commenting on everything he saw out of the window as the train slowed to a near stop.

"Look at that guy with the broom. Shouldn't he be cleaning up? Instead, he's having his espresso right in the middle of the day! There's plenty to clean up. Let's hope we get going very soon." He didn't seem to notice how interesting it was that the man's broom was different from the standard version—made of thin pieces of cane bent in a moon-shaped semicircle.

He then turned to me. "I bet you're excited about the World Cup, eh? But look, look, look at this city."

Directing his attention back to the sweeper, he mouthed through the window, "Take your time with that espresso. You have all day and you can clean up tomorrow. There will be more things for you to sweep anyway. Why bother sweeping up now, anyway. Good for you. Enjoy the espresso."

When the train finally stopped, my mother and I got up to take the bags from the overhead compartment, and the man gave us a surprised look."

"You're getting off here? I see, I see. Well, well, have a good stay. Good wishes for you."

I had never heard any Italians speak of Naples with such obvious disdain; a few subtle remarks were the most I had heard before, such as, "It might be difficult to find a taxi in Naples. The bus drivers don't keep on schedule."

When I got off the train, I was feeling intense dislike for my seatmate, but I also began to wonder whether his remarks held any truth at all. I began to survey the station people closely. The men in carts, coming to the side of the train to sell sandwiches and drinks to the passengers were holding up drinks and tapping on the windows with them. The railroad employees were walking around in their gray-blue closed-collared jackets. Their small, brown leather pocketbooks, full of tickets and coins, were tied around their waists, resting on their bellies. Here and there along a wall were women sitting with outstretched hands, asking for coins.

The man with the broom had finished his espresso and was now sweeping the floor in long, smooth strokes.

"Yes, maybe it is a little dirtier than Rome or Genova or Florence," I said to myself. "But so what? It's a wonderful city anyway."

When we got out of the station, a few taxi drivers and a woman selling little dolls hanging from a stick accosted us. We chose a taxi driver and asked him to bring us to the Via Egiziaca a Pizzofalcone. He was wearing only a T-shirt on top, and mounds of hair were sticking out of the shirt at his shoulders. The driver was silent for the first part of the ride but then started talking nonstop.

"It's going to be some World Cup," he reported enthusiastically. "We have some good ones this year. We will have to watch out for England and the Charlton brothers, Brazil and Pelé, and Germany with Haller. But Fachetti is ours. He will be dangerous to stop. He is playing defense but suddenly he will be jutting forward and pah! The ball will be put on Rivera's foot or maybe Mazzola's."

I knew the players because posters with their names were plastered all over the walls, their pictures were in the magazines and papers, and I had been collecting little "stamps" with their pictures. I nodded a few times to show that I was listening, but it didn't seem to matter to the taxi driver. He continued as if he were talking to himself.

"Yes, this is going to be quite a Cup. Eusebio is from Mozambique but plays for Portugal. Is it fair? Is it? I'm just asking a simple question, little one, what do you say? Is it fair?"

I looked a little confused and wasn't sure what to say, but he kept urging me to answer.

"It's not that I'm asking you if you can perform surgery on my liver. It's just a simple question. What do you think?"

"I don't think it's fair," I replied cautiously. "No, not really, but I don't know for sure."

"Yes, you're right, it's not fair, but those are the rules. I didn't make them up or at least no one asked me about the rules. I'm just a guy from Naples with a car that blows too much black smoke. And I have an opinion. Should I shoot myself because I have an opinion?"

When we got home, he urged me to root very hard for Italy. "We have to do our best for this rotten team. Too bad the games are in England. I mean, who can perform well in that English air? We'll have to root very hard. Chile is coming up in a few days. Root very hard, little one. Let's send Chile back to Chile."

When I got home, I asked my Nonno about Italy and what he thought.

"I think Rivera sprained his leg. Who knows?"

Then I told my grandmother and Aunt Adele about the man on the train.

"They love to pick on the Napoletani," said my grandmother, shaking her head sadly.

Aunt Adele seemed more disturbed. "If the man had gotten off the train and walked around town, he would have seen that there is nothing different here from anywhere else. There are a few strange people like anywhere else. They always say that Neapolitans are this and that, but listen to me. As far as work goes, the Neapolitan works. In fact, the Neapolitan is one of the best workers. It's a fact that is well recognized."

That night I asked my Aunt Ada about Italy's chances for the World Cup.

"And what do I know? What am I, an expert about soccer?" she asked dismissively, turning back to her paper.

I then asked her about the man who spoke badly of Naples.

She responded huffily, "Let him come to my office and he can work there. We'll see if he can keep up with the work. There's no use talking to them. They have a fixed idea and so it remains."

The next morning I went down to the courtyard, where I found Pasquale watering the plants. He had a little watering pail and had to walk back to a spigot near the entrance of the courtyard each time it was emptied and then go back to the fortunate plant he was watering.

"Why don't you use a bigger pail to water the plants?" I asked.

"It's good for my legs to walk, especially in the mornings. That's when the muscles in the legs have to be extended for the work of the day. And then, where am I going? Do I have an important meeting with the president of the United States?"

I walked back and forth with him and asked him about Italy's chances for the World Cup.

"I'm afraid it's not good this time. We have a team that plays in the old-fashioned style, waiting, waiting, waiting for the perfect pass in front of the goal. The long pass. The long cross in front. Teams no longer play that way. The Brazilians use short passes, tic-e-tac, tic-e-tac, and before you know it they are in front of the goal. These long passes will not win the big games. You can't count on them. Tic-e-tic and tac, tac, and right onto the goal. That's how to play."

He then put his hand on my shoulder as the water spilled out from the pail to the side. "Listen to me. We have no Pelé. Mazzola is not Pelé. That's just the way it is. I don't wish it to be that way. Of course, it would be nice if the Azzurri won all the time, but we have to face what is a fact. They will not be good this year."

I then told him about the man on the train and he looked a little more serious.

"Let me water this tree here and then meet me right on that step," he said, pointing to the step in question.

After he emptied the water and brought the pail back to his house, he came over to me. "You said that the man on the train was complaining about Naples. Was he from Milan by any chance?"

"He didn't say," I answered.

"Did he give any clue as to where he was from? For instance, did he say the r's from his throat without the real roll at the tip of the tongue. That might mean he was from Torino."

"I don't think so. What if he was from Milan?"

"Ahhh. Well, first of all, Robertino, let me tell you that I have heard this Neapolitan thing my whole life. I'm not deaf. But let me tell you about the Milanese. They think they are from a big, important city and not one that is part of Italy. It's European," he said, exaggerating the length of each syllable of the word "Eu-ro-pe-an."

He continued, now flushed with emotion. "But this is what he doesn't realize. He walks around like a big man be-cause he is from Milan, but he is big only in his own mind. What does anyone else give a damn where he is from? From Torino, it's just as bad. The Torinese walks around saying to himself, 'I am from the big, industrialized city of Torino.' And who gives a damn except himself? And the Roman—he walks around saying to himself, 'Io sono dalla capitale.' [I am from the capital city.] As for the Neapolitan, yes, he can be a lazy bastard and say, 'Why should I bust my chops? So I can have the big Lancia instead of the Fiat?' But the Neapolitan can work better than anyone. Give a Neapolitan a shovel and he will dig you a hole to China."

Over the next few days more posters of the players and the team were plastered on the walls of the buildings, cars were driving around with Italian flags, and the talk in all the café's was about soccer, soccer, soccer. The news consisted primarily of updates on the condition of all the players and how they had looked in practice.

My Uncle Bruno played it cool, but I could tell he was excited too. He was talking with his friends and even the lady in the tobacco shop about the Chile game.

I, however, was very worried. I could not get the phrase, "The old-fashioned style" out of my mind. I did not dare bring up the problem with the long passes and the tic-e-tac style of Brazil that could get the ball in front of the goal in no time. If this was true, how could Italy win? I talked with Uncle Bruno about the players and the game but never brought up the problem of the long passes or the waiting for the perfect pass in front of the goal.

It was hard to sleep the night before the Chile game. I woke up several times and looked at the clock. I divided the hours in halves, then in quarters. It seemed that the next day would never come and that I would be eleven years old forever.

Italy won the first game 2–0! When the game ended, cars honked their horns, boats blew their whistles, and flags were flying from windows and cars. Small groups of people walked through the streets singing. Even late that night, horns and yells punctured the silence every few minutes.

Pasquale was cautiously pleased when I saw him, and I wondered if he might have been wrong about the old style of play. "*Vedremo, vedremo*" (We'll see, we'll see), he muttered.

There was a tangible sense of happiness all over Naples. People were a little louder, and talk in the cafés was nonstop soccer. On the Pizzofalcone, the men who sat in chairs in front of their homes were eager to call me over and talk soccer. "This is how you play soccer, Robertino. You're seeing how it should be done. There are some tough games ahead, but we are in good shape," the pesci-vendolo (fish-seller) told me.

For the next two days I forgot all about the problems with the long passes and the "superior" style of the Brazilians. But in the next game disaster struck. Russia beat Italy 1–0. The offense was bad and the Russian goalie was terrific. Immediately the mood was somber. A blanket of silence descended on the city. In the Gambrinus Café the man who made the espressos was arguing with a patron.

"It's obvious that we are not good. The offense cannot do it. Fachetti needs to bring the ball further up to midfield," and he put down a cup he had just finished cleaning. "And where was Bulgarelli? Did you see him do anything?"

Giuseppino was sitting in his wicker chair when I came back up the Pizzofalcone. As I walked by, he said nothing but just puckered his lips and brought both hands up to his face with his palms facing upward to say, "What are you going to do?"

Pasquale told me that this was exactly what he had worried about. The first game might have been a fluke, and the old style of play had really "bitten them in the ass." Fortunately, he said, North Korea was the next opponent and was very weak

Uncle Bruno was more optimistic; he said that Lev Yashin, the Russian goalie, was the best in the world and it was naturally very difficult to score against him; he knew that Italy would win over North Korea and then they had a good chance of beating the next team.

The North Korea game was three days later. That morning I went to buy rolls at the panificio (bakery), and my friend the baker was in a good mood. I asked for six rolls as usual, and as he put them in a bag, he gave each roll a name:

"Fachetti," he pronounced, dropping one roll in the bag.

"Mazzola," he continued, dropping another one in.

"Albertosi—let's hope he can do the job," he implored, and dropped another one in.

That day I did not even watch the game, caught up in the optimism of all around me. I was in the courtyard waiting until the end of the game, at which time I planned to run down the street with everyone cheering, but when I didn't hear any whistles blowing or people screaming, I became worried. I looked down the desolate street; not even the "usuals" were sitting in their chairs.

Mrs. Malvese was the first to appear in the courtyard. She had a small folding chair that she opened up and was carrying a basket full of string beans. She sat down and started pulling the ends of the string beans and throwing them in the basket. After a minute she turned to me and said, "They lost, Robertino." I was stunned and she must have seen it. "That's the way it goes, Robertino. Time to prepare the beans. Even if they won, I would still have to prepare these beans," she laughed.

Pasquale came out of the little door that led to his room and walked slowly over to me. "We have to keep up with the modern way of doing things and we just don't know how. The long passes didn't work, so the outcome isn't that unbelievable. The short passes are what gets the job done, not this slow way. And that's the end of it. The good thing is that now we don't have to worry anymore. We can relax and enjoy the remaining games."

That night Uncle Bruno came by and patted me on the head. "Did you see? Did you see what our big team did? We have no Yascin, we have no Eusebio, we have no Pelé."

Giuseppino took the loss hard. "We have failed very badly. We couldn't come through even against Korea. *Che vergogna, che vergogna.*" (What a shame, what a shame.)

Naples was much quieter the next day. I walked down the street, through the Piazza Plebiscito and down to the port.

There was a little less exuberance in the "Buon giornos" and most people were in no mood for lengthy conversations. At the port, tourists were running for the ferry boats to Capri and Ischia, and the "coconut man" was calling out for everyone to look at the beautiful coconuts he had for sale. "Coco fresco, coco fresco," he yelled, holding small sample slices in his outstretched hand.

The high-pitched beeps of cars rang out, and the crackle of sparks from the overhead cables of electric trams stung the air. As I was looking at a poster of the Italian team, someone came by and ripped it right off with one hand as he walked by, leaving part of it still on the wall and the remainder in shreds. They flew into the air, then settled in the street.

Within days, no one talked any more about the game with North Korea. The streets resumed their normal life, and a few words here and there were said about the other teams. The posters were all down, and the normal hum of the city resumed. The baker baked his rolls and gave me some. Giuseppino wanted to know why there was no good bread in America, and Pasquale watered the trees with his pail. Life had returned to normal.

I thought of the man who had looked at Naples with his nose to the train window and had wanted to speedily be on his way. How much he was missing, I thought, and how happy I was that Naples had been my destination.

Chapter Elveven

The Bombola Man and Other Shopping Adventures

The voices of singing salesmen greeted every summer morning on the streets of Naples. Like birds answering each other's calls, so did these songs of fruits, fish, and wares for sale resonate through the city streets.

"Fresh blackberries, just hand picked this morning. Come and get them before they're gone," the Blackberry Man would urge every morning at 7:00 A.M., his voice echoing from the stone walls of the buildings.

Next came the Fresh Egg Man. "They're still warm from the chicken's body. I have only good, big ones. Get 'em right here." Sometimes my grandmother would yell out the window that he should come up.

"Buon giorno, Signora," he would say, entering the house. "They are especially large today."

"Si, si," my grandmother would respond. "Let's have a look at them." The Fresh Egg Man would carefully swing his wicker basket under my grandmother's face and slowly lift the white sheet covering the precious eggs.

"Give me these four right here, and don't switch them. These four," she would say, pointing firmly at her prized choices.

Once a week the Olive Oil Man would sing in the street, warbling about the beautiful, clear olive oil he carried in the tin jugs balanced on a stick across his back. He would fill any jar of your choice with the prized oil and then hold it up to the light for inspection. It was always clear and perfect—at least according to him.

Then there was the Bombola Man, who brought us compressed gas in heavy metal canisters to run the stove. He would come in and secure the new canister in place, flinging the old, empty one over his shoulder and stumbling out the door. The Bombola Men whizzed through Naples in their Lambrettas, always headed toward another customer, a canister strapped to each side of their scooters.

Anywhere you walked in Naples was likely to be the site of yet another sales "opportunity of a lifetime." Someone was always selling something. My mother and Nonno knew that if they walked with me, even though I was only eight, I would have to stop to watch demonstrations of the latest gizmos and gadgets. How I longed to buy every one of them!

One day we came upon a man in front of a large crowd, spouting what seemed to be political diatribe. But upon closer scrutiny, we saw that he was demonstrating an incredible thingamajig. He held it up for all to see, majestically, as if it were the sword that had slain Achilles. A small, silvery, spoon-sized object, it was apparently a wondrous tool capable of taking on infinite chores, a super Swiss army knife worthy of James Bond himself. It could cut glass, open cans, sharpen knives, split bricks in half, and puncture practically anything, the salesman announced with confidence.

He then performed all the tasks with perfection, easily cutting what seemed to be a windowpane with one easy gesture. All this time he spoke of the object's virtues, including its durability—it would last for many years—as well as its compact design. "No one can afford to be without one!"

he insisted, and I had to agree. Then he sang a song to the tune of "O Sole Mio" about how, if you bought these magical utensils for friends and relatives, you would one day receive commensurate gifts in return.

I wanted one of these amazing all-purpose tools. The feats the man, performed with the little object demonstrated such infinite usage that purchasing one seemed an excellent investment. How could Nonno possibly object to my having an object of such utility?

I bought it with my own money. The price—200 lire, or 30 cents—seemed rather steep, but well worth it. It was shaped like a flat fish, made out of metal, and was about four inches long. On the "face" end of the fish was a little wheel for glass cutting. I slipped it into my pocket and couldn't wait to get home to use it.

Later that afternoon, while everyone was napping, I tried to cut off a small corner of my grandmother's glass coffee table. To my disappointment, I wasn't successful. The little wheel squeaked and turned around innocently, making a few scratches on the surface of the glass. But that was it. The amazing, all-purpose tool didn't do any of the other things it was supposed to either. I tried not to be too disappointed that my spectacular purchase was a failure. Fortunately, everyone seemed to have forgotten that I had bought it and never asked me any questions about it.

That afternoon, gazing at my purchase in puzzlement, I recalled the salesman's performance and wondered what he had used to perform his magic. His impressive show had only served to magnify my bitterness. How I had longed to make my own magic with the tool, and how deeply I felt my inability to realize the expectations I had so innocently nurtured on my way home.

—w—

I had a very different experience the following year. My Aunt Lietta, aged ninety, announced that she would like to buy me a book. As the customary goodbye gift at the end of my visit—a ricordo, or remembrance, of that summer.

Aunt Lietta was referred by most of my relatives as a "fine and classy lady," as was the custom in the fancy language often used in that era's Italian. She seemed that way to me, too, in the best sense of the word. Aunt Lietta may have been old and frail, but she was always elegant and mild-mannered.

Although she told me that she had made an appointment with a bookseller, I had not thought much of it, and certainly did not think that the purchase of a book would be an event in itself. But it was.

I got a hint of what was to come when, at the appointed time, my aunt appeared in the courtyard in an elegant silk dress and told me that we would be taking an automobile to the store.

A few minutes later a large black sedan was outside in the street; the driver, in a tuxedo and white gloves, got out of the car and opened the door for us. "I hope everything is to your liking, Signora," he said.

When we arrived at an old building with huge, sparkling clean windows, the proprietor of the store was waiting for us at the door and accompanied us to a private room on the second floor. He moved and spoke with an elegance and effeminate grace seen only in black-and-white movies—the kind featuring lovers sparring at Manhattan supper clubs.

"Please, do have a seat," he urged us respectfully. We sat down at a large wooden, antique desk, where we waited a few moments while he retrieved some books for our inspection. He laid out a few of them on a velvet cloth and quietly retreated to another room.

To my surprise, they were all art books. Aunt Lietta leafed through a few of them, pointing out the pictures. "This one looks very nice and this other one has excellent reproductions. Which one would you desire to have, Roberto?"

I picked a set of three bound in a cardboard case, and my aunt called for the proprietor, who quickly approached us and picked up my selections. We were then brought into another room, this one paneled in dark, English-boarding-school wood, where the books were wrapped carefully and with great fanfare.

When we left the store, the limousine driver was waiting to bring us back home. As we drove home, I couldn't resist looking at my wrapped present, and then at my Aunt Lietta. "What a lovely way to buy a book," I thought, and how I loved my Aunt Lietta for being her very elegant, generous self.

—m—

"La Forcella" in Naples is a section of winding streets and, at least to my twelve-year-old way of thinking, of sleazy, disreputable, desperate, conniving characters who would sell their mothers and sisters if the price were right. Even though my visits were infrequent, I loved going there. Just hearing the word "Forcella" brought a rush of excitement, as if I were to be given five minutes to walk invisibly through a genuine whorehouse.

It was no doubt a neighborhood like many others, with perfectly normal children and even adults going about their business. But I had heard talk of the mysterious ways of its vendors, the "Camorra" types who lived there, and the unscrupulous merchants who would sell counterfeit Parker pens and Zippo lighters. Going there, I thought, was like going to Times Square to buy a camera, recognizing that you would be made a sucker, that you would get home, open your box with that glossy picture of the Pentax you wanted, only to find a stone in place of the expected camera.

Going to La Forcella to buy anything was tantamount to gambling. In the hopes of saving a little money, you were willingly stepping into a quagmire of deceit, into a den of thieves, into a bazaar of bad characters. Nevertheless, we went, my Uncle Bruno and I. We went in order to buy me the walkie-talkies I had been dreaming about ever since my friend Stuart had gotten a pair from his father, who worked at a camera store and got them "cheap."

Bruno was like my second father, taking delight in the childlike musings of my youth, in the true stories and exaggerations I would tell, and in the slapstick routines that I believed displayed my thespian talents. He loved it all because he had the spark of a child in him too. Venturing in La Forcella to buy me anything at all was a true sign that he loved me. However, it was also a dubious indication of his prowess as a discriminating consumer.

Bruno had gotten a tip from a colleague about exactly where to go, and now he walked with determination and conviction into a small store where cameras and other gadgets hung on the outer door, draped as if on a Christmas tree. With confidence he said, "Buon giorno. I would like to buy a pair of walkie-talkies for my nephew here."

"You have come to the right place," the salesman replied, "but we must ask some questions to make sure you receive the proper model for your needs. What will the young man be using them for?"

Hmmm. I thought about how I might use the walkie-talkies when spying or when reporting my neighbors' suspicious behavior.

"Just for fun," I said.

"Then yes, you will still need a good pair that will last you a lifetime and you will get quality use out of it. Take a look at what I have here." Hanging on the wall were walkie-talkies of various sizes, shapes, and colors. I picked out a silver pair, not too small and not too plastic-looking.

"I see the young man has good taste and really knows quality. Those are excellent, a very fine pair, a little expensive but well worth the money. In fact, that pair would make an excellent investment. They are only 35,000 [$55]."

Uncle Bruno looked shaken, even a bit depressed. "I was thinking I could get a pair like that for about 15,000," he said unconvincingly. "The most I would pay is 20,000 for them."

The salesman looked suddenly stricken, almost para-lyzed, as if he were a wild beast hit with a poisoned dart. The lines of his face became more defined as he slowly sat down, steadying himself after hearing the tragic news of so low an offer.

"This is not possible, signore, not for this pair. This is a very fine pair. Perhaps as a favor to the boy I could let you have these for 30,000."

This was not a good game for Bruno. He not only was uncomfortable, but clearly felt out of his element. He looked at me sidewise, not wanting to disappoint me. I appreciated his dilemma, but not enough to forfeit my desire to attain the coveted pair. I could actually see myself holding them, run-ning around calling to my friends, telling them where I was and asking for instructions from the "home base."

Bruno looked more and more pained. There are people for whom the world of trade, barter, and commerce is an im-position on their gentle nature, and who feel the unpleasant effects of confrontation long after the event is over. Such was my gentle uncle.

While he was nervous at the thought of objecting to the absurdly high price, he was driven by necessity to try to lower it. This I could tell from his hesitations and faltering speech;

he clearly cowed in the presence of a man who did this for a living. While Bruno wasn't clever enough to be anything but his honest, kindhearted self, he was too genuine to play at being unmoved by the battle being played out with him as a key participant.

He and the salesman made several attempts, false starts, and halfhearted gestures toward a compromise, a fair meeting point where the two bargainers might leave each other with a semblance of dignity and satisfaction culminating in the successful purchase of the desired walkie-talkies. At one point a weighty silence filled the crowded little room, a moment of well-deserved repose before the final and decisive push toward resolution.

With one final, desperate attempt, blurted out from the depth of his lungs, Bruno managed to scream out, "25,000!" And that was the number that his combatant could not resist. The salesman collapsed in his chair, slumped to one side dejectedly, as if hearing that his wife of thirty years had birthed two children with his bastard brother. He clutched his two hands slowly toward his heart, sadly squeezing his shirt in deliberate, convulsive bursts. "Your hard bargaining has given me a heart pain. I need a moment to recover, to gain my equilibrium. I think I will be okay."

We waited patiently, and after a slight pause he said, "You have a deal, signore. At this price it is like giving them away but I am in no mood to make a counteroffer or to resist you. Would you like them in their original box or may I simply wrap them in paper?"

On the way home, in the car, I could see the box in the backseat. I pretended it was any ordinary box and this was any ordinary day. But deep inside, I was drinking from an elixir of joy as I observed the scenes and sounds on the road streaming past my window. The very cacophony of trucks and cars, of children playing ball, and of women selling their goods became an orchestrated crescendo of blissful sounds.

In a short time I would be holding one of the walkie-talkies while talking from the moon or one of the outer planets to Houston, figuring out how to describe the wonders I was seeing. In reality, I would soon be reporting to my Uncle Bruno, sitting on the terrace below, about the condition of the stale bread to be used for making bread crumbs left in a cotton sack hanging on the kitchen door. No matter. I was bringing the walkie-talkies home to the United States with me. Would they work at sea between the lido and promenade decks?

During the next few days, secret conversations took place between my brother and me, and Uncle Bruno and me. One or the other was usually at the home base—my grandmother's dining room—as I roamed the rest of the house or ventured into the garden to report on meteorological conditions or the comings and goings of suspicious characters in the courtyard. Most of the conversations, however, consisted of saying, "Can you hear me? Can you hear me now? Can you still hear me?"

There are moments in a boy's life when the very planets seem to be aligned in his favor and all is right in his life. Such were my first few days of walkie-talkie ownership. I was a keen observer of the social scene occurring in the gardens below my grandmother's house. I noted the actions of my grandmother's neighbors as they "innocently" went about their routines, picking up mail, walking in and out of their apartments as if these acts were all in the normal scheme of things. Urgently I reported back to the home base about these and numerous other happenings, recognizing that others were waiting for this important news.

But just as events were proceeding in harmony with my childish desires, disappointment struck as quickly and decisively. The walkie-talkies stopped working. It was not the

batteries, for new ones were put in. It was an actual break-
down, a total functional noncompliance. This was a drastic
and totally unexpected turn of events.

In my despair, I played with the receiver button endlessly, hoping that a small tap to it might set things right. I
tapped and secretly begged the walkie-talkie gods to repair
what was wrong. I moved the antenna to different positions
and screamed to the now dejected Bruno, "Can you hear
me? Can you hear me?" All attempts availed nothing.

I must have seemed as desperate as a homeless man buying lotto tickets to correct his life. Up to this point I had
been filled with woe at the thought of not having the little
talking machines to play with. However, Bruno's mood indicated the real crisis that was looming in the near future.
We would have to return to the scene of the sale, despite the
expense involved in returning them to the godfather of elec-
tronics. This meant a venture once again into La Forcella, a
prospect that I anticipated with as much gloom as if I were
about to traverse the river Styx with Mephistopheles himself
as the oarsman.

That week Bruno was Prince Hamlet, hesitating, inquiring about alternatives to seeing his former nemesis again,
stuck in the quicksand of doubt, spinning in a quandary
of perplexity; anything would be better than returning the
walkie-talkies. We could measure his stress by his anxious
stabs at finally making a decision.

I despaired, thinking that the best avenue was that of least
resistance, to simply forgo the pleasures of wireless commu-
nication and spare poor Bruno his mental anxiety. That week
I had a foretaste of the toll that mental anxiety takes on the
mind, its capacity to drain the spirit, a condition I would experience many times later in life. In a burst of generosity, I decided to tell Bruno not to return the walkie-talkies. This would
be the only way to release both of us from further pain.

For several days we put the task aside and ignored facing up to the unpleasant consequences. But Uncle Bruno decided that it had to be done soon, or the very passage of time would be excuse enough to deny us our rightful claim to a new, or at least repaired pair, of taking machines.

So one hot morning Uncle Bruno and I began our trek to the salesman's shop, as silent as condemned prisoners being led to the gallows. He was undoubtedly thinking of several scenarios that might undo his plans, for he was concentrating with that undiluted ferocity that one might see on a grandmaster chess champion about to spring his supreme move on an opponent.

We were greeted cordially on our arrival, despite my noticing that the man had seen me holding the little gray machines in my hand and therefore must have known our purpose in coming. But he played dumb, wanting to hear us before issuing a response.

Bruno began by announcing that the machines did not work and we would like him to have a look at them and see what he could do. The man took this news in stride, but I was not fooled; he was preparing a strategy for what he knew would be an inevitable showdown. He casually gazed at the walkie-talkies, poked around, and opened the back of them, appearing to examine the product in order to appease us. Yet we both knew he had no intention of helping us.

"Unfortunately they are broken and unfortunately there is little I can do about it. All sales are final, and besides, I have no way of knowing how they came to be broken. I am very sorry."

It might have been judicious, given Bruno's inclination toward high blood pressure and the rate of heart disease running in the family, to step back and let things be, to accept the inequities of this world with resignation and willingly submit to circumstances. After all, the ways of God's handiwork remain mysterious, and one may find comfort in knowing that the wheel of fortune spins as it might, although one may always hope it will land on one's lucky number soon.

However, Bruno was thinking along quite different lines, for he exploded in a tirade of reproach and admonition worthy of an angry God beholding a disobedient supplicant.

Alas it was all to no avail. I was still holding the objects about which all the fuss was being made with little hope of even getting them out of my grasp. In the middle of this gritty exchange, which was now settling down to a mere quarrel, a slight woman stepped in the room with two small espressos on a tray and offered each of the combatants one.

"How many sugars?" she asked Bruno before handing him the diminutive cup.

"Just two, thank you" he said before stepping back to ask me what time it was, then telling me that upon leaving he would buy me an ice cream. Both men welcomed the peaceful interlude, for they had to recharge their batteries for the next round. The woman now sat in a corner and had the imploring look of one pleading for mercy for her son.

"Do not overtax my poor son's heart," she seemed to say through her silence. Bruno had fought the good fight, and although he had not brought home the enemy's head on a platter, neither had his own head been left in the man's store on a pole. For now, we would have to leave La Forcella with the two broken walkie-talkies, comforted in the knowledge that possibly another day would come when the fight would be carried to the enemy more forcefully and conclude victoriously.

A few days later we were back. This time the espressos were brought out immediately, an excellent negotiating strategy for both parties. A more civil discussion ensued, including tangential, and to my mind irrelevant, topics. This time the salesman's resistance was lessened considerably, worn away as if by attrition. He probably wanted the issue settled before he ran out of coffee.

In a last attempt to "save face," he repeated his side of the story. Bruno listened graciously, now sure that he would prevail. By the time we left the store, I was in a golden haze, holding two new walkie-talkies. In hindsight, the whole encounter was enjoyable, the screaming a façade, the yelling merely dramatic artifice. In short, I had witnessed and survived a commonplace yet glorious battle in the trenches of Neapolitan commerce.

Chapter Twelve

—ɯ—

La Strada

On many mornings our family would go to one of the beaches along the gulf outside the city. To get there, we had to walk down a series of steep steps from the Via Pizzofalcone to the Piazza Plebiscito, where we could catch a bus. Thankfully, several landings interrupted these stairs.

Occupying one of the landings sat Signor Di Stefano. It was difficult to walk anywhere in Naples without encountering beggars, petty entrepreneurs, and self-appointed service workers. They were of all ages, from the young *scugnizzi* (ragamuffins) to the very old.

Signor Di Stefano awaited us every day in his regulation gray suit, red tie, black shoes, and cane in hand. Tucked away in a hole in the wall just behind him was his bagged lunch, and all who encountered him would be greeted by a sign reading, "I am blind. Please help me. Your humble friend, Signor Di Stefano."

Into his small cup we would drop a few coins, and in time he began to recognize us. After thanking us, he often asked why we hadn't walked by the previous day, on those rare occasions when we hadn't gone to the beach. When we were late, he would tell us to hurry up or we would miss the boat, and when we were early he would advise us to slow down, since the boat would not be leaving for a while.

Signor Di Stefano always sat upright and had a surprisingly cheerful disposition, as if life had dealt him a good hand after all. He had few facial wrinkles and looked like a man in his late fifties who had lived an abundant life. The lines in his face looked as if they had been sculpted there with great care, resting naturally along the curves of his nose and around his cheekbones.

I took comfort in Signor Di Stefano's steady presence; like the light, he appeared every day, and to a child, continuity keeps the darkness away. When we came home in the early afternoon, weary travelers, hungry and hot from the blazing sun, Signor Di Stefano would no longer be in his spot, although his chair still remained, now folded and tied to a railing.

One day we were coming home earlier than usual, and I noted that a young woman, perhaps his daughter, was helping Signor Di Stefano rise and put away his chair. He seemed to be in pain, and because he was heavy, the girl strained to hold his weight against her body as she folded the chair with one hand.

Struggling forward, trying to walk, the man limped heavily, leaning to one side. I suddenly realized that, before he had become a beggar, this man had lived a life apart from that of a lone figure awaiting possible benefactors on these steep stairs. Could it be that the money dropped into his cup was all he had? Was it his only source of potential food and rent? Was he supporting a family we weren't even aware of?

On that momentous day Signor Di Stefano's pain and blindness made him stumble enough to show me how out of harmony he actually was with his surroundings. His dignified demeanor while he was perched on the stairs had shielded me from the reality of his situation—a man sitting in a chair on a landing on hot summer days, with a cup and a cane in his hands. His serene personality had led me to interpret his gentle greeting as the sign of a tranquil, satisfying life. Clearly this man had a more complex history than I had imagined.

Although we saw him often after this occasion, it was the only time he ever revealed anything amiss. For years Signor Di Stefano occupied the same landing on those summer mornings. He always greeted us in the same manner, thanking us for putting a few coins in his cup. There was little sign that he had aged much, except for a slightly curved back, which I observed the last time I saw him, in 1968, when I walked by Piazza Plebiscito.

It was my grandmother who told me how Signor Di Stefano had lost his mobility. Apparently he had been a victim of the bombings during World War II. I wondered how many other Signor Di Stefanos wandered the country, maimed in body or soul—or both—from the war.

Although the day finally arrived when he no longer occupied his place on the landing, he would always remain in my mind as a lone figure in a gray suit, matching the gray of the stony ground upon which he sat.

—∞—

By all accounts Arturo was "a lazy, no-good son-of-a-bitch bastard." He sold cigarettes in a small street just off the Via Roma, where two cardboard boxes were balanced to form a small, improvised table. Since my Nonno smoked two packs a day, he needed cigarettes all the time, and Arturo supplied them cheaply.

Nonno told me many stories about how Arturo came to be in his current circumstances. He had been a sailor, he had been in jail, and he had come to Naples after leaving his wife in another city. All the different accounts of Arturo's life were contradictory, but as long as they pointed to his unsavory qualities, they were accurate enough. It was the gist of his life, rather than its actual details, that Nonno wanted to impress upon me.

Arturo sold Marlboros, Camels, Lucky Strikes, and some foul-smelling English things that he somehow obtained from sailors. Every time we walked by to pick up a couple of packs, he would terrify me with his black eyes and demonic, three-toothed grin. He sat on a little stool behind his boxes, where, from a sack behind him, he would pull out whichever brand of cigarettes you wanted.

According to Arturo, he had a difficult job, which he complained about incessantly.

"The weather sucks. My suppliers are late. This city is going to the dogs. Do you think it's easy acquiring this merchandise so I can give it away to you?"

But none of this mattered to Nonno. He happily took the soft packs of Marlboros, put them in his pockets, and, when we left, laughed at all of Arturo's troubles.

"He's a petty thief, Roberto. He's handsome too. Did you see his teeth?"

"Why buy from him?" I asked. "Aren't there others who sell cigarettes?"

"I buy from him because he sells cheap. He keeps raising the price though. A few teeth would suit him well, eh?"

When we got home, Nonno pulled out a Marlboro from the soft pack. When he lit, the sparks touched the curtain flowing in the breeze outside, making yet another little hole in the curtain. All the little holes looked like a map of the night sky.

"Lousy cigarettes," he yelled. "Lousy, thief bastard."

Professor Sanucci was not affiliated with any university;

rather he was a "philosopher" who occupied a portion of the street I would occasionally pass near the port. He had a long white beard, his small eyes darted to the side, and he sat on the ground in an old black suit. In front of him was a small wooden crate, which was once used to ship fruit and which he had adapted into a small desk. Small, sliding pieces of cardboard served as drawers and held pieces of paper and newspaper articles. A small nameplate on the box read, "Professore Sanucci." To one side of the professor's desk was a dish in which passersby were encouraged to drop coins.

Professor Sanucci dispensed opinions of all sorts on almost any topic. I remember him mostly engaging in diatribes against the "establishment," complaining that "our leaders have betrayed the people. They are only in politics for their own good." He urged people not to vote for any politician and to kick the present "bums" out. Occasionally he would take out one of the pieces of paper from his drawer and read a few lines of a magazine article that buttressed his own opinion.

Once I saw him addressing a small group of tourists about the wonders of coconut milk and encouraging all who listened to drink it every evening. "It's better than wine or mother's milk," he said. And sure enough, after fumbling around in his "desk," he produced an exposé on the wonders of coconut milk, as if to show that others concurred with his opinion.

Professor Sanucci was quiet when alone, but when people walked by he tried to "reel them in" with his eyes, staring straight at them until they acknowledged his presence. If they did so for even a second, he went straight into his "lecture," hoping that they would be lured nearer to listen and to drop coins into his dish.

One day my Nonno gave me a coin to drop in his dish as we walked past him. We were in a hurry and had no desire to stop to hear his lecture, so I started walking away just as the professor began to rant about how corrupt the world was. When I turned away from him, he must have noticed that I didn't intend to stop, so he simply said, "Listen to what is right, and not what is wrong."

As an eleven-year-old, I hadn't the slightest idea what that meant or how to do it. Even today I wonder how one determines "right from wrong" on a moment's notice!

—◆—

Another enterprising gentleman with a box also worked near the port. A true Mr. Fix-It, he sat cross-legged behind a wooden carton that contained many small tools. He could repair all kinds of things: watches, shoes, handbags, eyeglasses, small radios, and other electronic gadgets. He was always busy when I saw him, and he must have been good, because people often waited in line to avail themselves of his services.

"Give me a little room. I need some space, please. Be patient, I'll be right with you," he would call out to the little crowd in front of him.

To assure his customers that he would always be found in his spot, he had written these words on the box:

"Office Hours: 8 A.M.—6 P.M. Monday–Saturday. Half day Sunday.

The firm of Mr. Ettore, Limited."

—◆—

I did not know her name, although I saw her on the same street for many years. She sat on the ground in front of the Standa department store with a small baby in her arms, one hand extended to accept a coin. Her long, loose black dress gave little indication of the body beneath it. She neither looked anyone in the face nor ever spoke a word that I could hear.

Sometimes the "Standa woman" had different children with her. A little boy with her once had what seemed to be a burn on his face and another had no arms. Another time, a little girl with a scarred face paced up and down in front of her, looking lost and sad. My aunt told me that this woman probably paid mothers desperate for cash to use their children as props to attract sympathy for her "plight." However, most people simply walked past the "Standa woman" without giving her or the child she was with any notice, except for occasionally stepping to the side to avoid coming too close to them.

There were other women like her, also with small, sometimes deformed, children sitting in different alleyways and along sidewalks in the shopping districts. Except for the children, they drew little attention to themselves. It frightened me to think that children could be taken away from their real parents and used in this manner, and it was shocking to learn that there were women who could make money only this way.

I remember resenting the woman in front of the Standa, and at the same time feeling guilty for resenting her. I understood the people who walked past her, wanting to make believe she didn't exist, but I also disliked the way each walker became blinded to her presence. In a city where many intruders stuck their noses in other people's business, this lack of attention unsettled me. Then again, I thought, shame and embarrassment can make others wish they were invisible. Was that what was happening here?

In years to follow, I would find many other examples of people averting their eyes to a scene they didn't wish to acknowledge. But for me, the "Standa woman" stands out, because she was my first encounter with the guilt that is manifested by avoiding others.

—ᴍ—

La Villa is a large public park along the bay near the center of Naples. It is an oblong oasis of tree-lined walkways just far enough from the busy road curving along the water to muffle the buzzing sounds of the legion of Fiats running through the city.

From one corner of the park begins the Via Chiaia, noted for its upscale stores. This small corner, between the park and Via Chiaia, was the domain of Luigi, a "freelance parking engineer."

He was easily spotted, with his ruddy skin, skeleton-thin body, and white cap that read, "Parking Supervisor." Whether we were going to the park or shopping, Luigi could make a parking spot appear where apparently there had been none. He would then park your car and watch over it for as much of the day as you wished, all for a mere 500 lire (80 cents). If you left him the key, he could move your car and thus accommodate others coming later. We trusted Luigi, and whenever we returned to pick up the car, it would be purring before us in just a few minutes.

Because he did what he did so artfully, no one cared that Luigi ruled over a section of street that was not a real parking area. Policemen passing by saluted him from their Alfa Romeos, and neighborhood residents waved at him affectionately.

Arranging for space was no easy feat for Luigi, but somehow he found a place for every vehicle placed in his care. Cars were put in every conceivable nook and cranny: some entirely on the sidewalk, others half on the sidewalk and half on the street. Some were parked between poles, others were inches from walls and other cars, or facing outward, inward, and sideways.

Luigi carried around a small ramp that he could lay down

to smoothly move cars up onto the sidewalk. He also had small blocks that he placed behind the front wheels to hold a car in place if it was on a steep incline.

Luigi never turned anyone away, no matter how many cars there were, seeming to defy physical law by creating new space where there was none. He worked hard constantly, in his own rhythm, getting keys, moving cars in and out of spots, and rearranging the cars that had not been picked up yet with the grace of a classical dancer. His body was the music, and the cars his orchestra.

When my Uncle Bruno and I arrived once in the middle of the day, distraught that there seemed to be little chance of finding a spot, Luigi called out to us, "Ingegniere, come here. There is always a spot for you." Bruno's generous "extra tips" were always appreciated. In a frenzy, cars moved in and out, backward and forward all over the street and rearranged like Legos to make a new space for Bruno's Lancia—ultimately his maneuverings were a miracle of geometrical arrangement.

Like so many in Naples, Luigi had made a job where there was none. At the end of one summer a younger, less skilled man was working the corner. He let us know that Luigi had moved on to a larger space near the Galleria. I was happy that he had been promoted, although I missed him very much. However, I knew that if we ever needed a parking spot near the Galleria...

—⚏—

The *scugnizzi* (little ragamuffins) of Naples were renowned for their survival techniques and resourcefulness. In the 1960s it was common to see many little boys roaming the streets, selling trinkets, assisting workers, or delivering drinks from the "bars," or coffeehouses. The deliverers could be seen all around town running with their little round trays, holding them in the air with one hand, espresso cups perfectly balanced on the tray. I remember two such boys very distinctly.

Silvio and his partner were very capable business associates. Silvio may have been ten, and his partner eight. Each wore a T-shirt, shorts, and plastic sandals. Silvio was clearly the boss, doing all the talking and blaring out orders to his cohort: "Go back and get the stuff," he would command impatiently. "Hand me the gold watch." "Let the gentleman see our beautiful merchandise."

The pair roamed the downtown city streets selling different items every day. Once they were in front of the post office, another time in front of the Upim department store. Sometimes they held packets of tissues that they sold for 100 lire (16 cents) and other times they sold *taralli* (peppery pretzels) or cotton handkerchiefs.

The boys not only approached you to show their wares, but they followed you for a few blocks, holding up in front of your face a "beautiful box of tissues." They let it be known that they had other items for sale as well. Noticing by our clothing that we may have been American, they called out to my father in English, "Do you need any kitchen items, glasses, shoes, or maybe a watch? I get for you." My father favored the tissues, while I always asked for the *taralli*. Once the boys held out a small Matchbox-type car with doors that really opened. They knew what a boy of their own age really craved. I tugged at my father's sleeve to buy me one, but he decided I should get one later at a real store.

One quiet Saturday morning my Uncle Bruno and I drove downtown to purchase a record of popular songs for me to bring back to New York. It had rained all night, but now the sun was out, the black-stoned streets had a wet sheen, and a cool breeze gently made its way through the streets. Between the buildings, a glimmer of blue Naples Bay could be seen with a few lazy sailboats bobbing up and down. It was one of those mornings when I was very happy to be alive.

We walked into a small record store, and after a brief consultation, the signorina brought out a record from the back of the store. She played it for my approval, wrapped it up and we were off. But when we got to the car, Uncle Bruno couldn't find his keys. We looked everywhere to no avail, and he became more and more agitated.

Just then Silvio and his partner appeared from nowhere. "I see you are having trouble there," he said with a touch of glee. "Can't find the keys, huh? Oh, my gosh, what are you going to do? You are stuck here."

We continued searching, under the car, in the street leading to the record store, in every pocket. All the while, Silvio seemed to take great delight in our dilemma. After a few minutes of our fumbling and growing frustration, we noticed that they were on the car seat. Sylvio leaned in to look inside the car too. He then called out, "Perhaps I can help you, sir?"

"What?" Bruno replied impatiently. "How can you help me?"

"Well, what year is that car, sir?"

"It's a 1964 Ondine. Not a Dauphine, an Ondine."

"The keys are the same."

"So?"

"I might be able to open the doors for you."

"How?" Uncle Bruno asked cautiously. "I don't want to break anything."

"Wait here. Just wait," Silvio replied. Turning to his partner, he said, "Let's go," and off they ran.

A few minutes later they were back, Silvio triumphantly holding up a large key ring, at least a foot in diameter, with dozens of dangling keys. "I have it, I have it," he declared triumphantly. He held the key up for us to admire, as if it were a fine wine, and then slipped it into the door lock and opened the door. "Pretty good, huh, for only 200 lire?"

"Yes, yes, very good, boys," Bruno said with relief, and gave him the money.

Silvio took the money and stood by the car smiling at us with great satisfaction. We got in and started to drive off, Uncle Bruno shaking his head.

"It's just crazy," Bruno was saying. "I don't get it. A key that opens every Ondine? How could there be such a thing? It's scary."

As we drove away, despite his misgivings about there being a key that could easily open his car—one produced so quickly by a little boy—I knew that Bruno was happy to be on his way home. I felt happy too that Silvio had come to our rescue, and that I now had a very valuable connection downtown, should I ever need it.

—m—

Garibaldi's name is ubiquitous in Italy; he was the great Italian military leader and liberator who unified his country in the nineteenth century. Naples has a Piazza Garibaldi with his statue in the middle, so the name has always lingered in my mind.

At the end of my grandparents' street, the Via Pizzofalcone, sat a bald man on a stoop whom I named "Gary Baldy." He sat mostly motionless, staring ahead while the life in front of him passed by. For some reason, he always called me over when I walked by, wanting to talk politics, about which, as a young boy, I knew absolutely nothing.

"Your President Johnson is a real Texas man," he would say, or "What do you think about Vietnam?"

I wouldn't say much more than "Si" or "Who knows?"

One day he asked me what I thought of Naples.

"I like it very much. I have a lot of family here." I said proudly.

"And America? Do you like that too?"

"Yes," I said, "I like that too," considering this a satisfactory answer.

"Do you really know Naples, what goes on here, between the beautiful bay and the Mount Vesuvio?"

I had no idea what he meant and asked, "What goes on here?"

"Roberto," he laughed in return, "can I come to America with you, maybe in a large valise, maybe this year when you go back?"

"Sure," I said, hoping this was only a joke, but not exactly certain.

"I might do it, I might, I really might," he half-promised, half-threatened.

One morning we were off to the beach, walking down Via Pizzofalcone, pails and shovels swinging from my hands. It was then that I saw Gary Baldy sitting on his stoop. I was hoping he wouldn't call me over, since I was thinking only of the beach and did not want to answer any questions about President Johnson. I didn't know whether to look his way, at least to say hello, or to just ignore him by pretending I was in deep conversation with my mother.

I decided to ignore him, but right after passing him, I felt bad and turned around to say hello. I was about to yell out Ciao when I saw him stretch out his empty hand to someone walking right behind us.

In an instant, I saw a look of extreme shame in his eyes as he pulled back his hand. I tried to make believe I had turned around to look up the street and not at him, but an awkward "Ciao" was already out of my mouth. Pivoting forward, I tried to convince myself that I hadn't seen the outstretched hand and therefore he would assume I hadn't seen it, either.

My uneasiness at having caught him begging left me worried all day. What would I say to him next time? Would he now ignore me or try to explain his actions?

Much to my relief, however, the next time I saw him nothing appeared different. Gary Baldy asked me if the United States and Russia would make peace and I said "Yes."

He laughed and said, "I hope so, Robertino, I hope so. For Jesus' sake, I hope so."

—∽—

Given that motels were nonexistent or too expensive for amorous rendezvous, lovers had no choice but to make love in their cars. All over Naples, in the corners of piazzas or at the dead end of streets, little Fiats were boarded up with pieces of cardboard on the inside pushing against the windows so nothing could be seen from the outside. They squeaked, shook, and rolled from the spirited lovemaking inside—and how I wished I could take a little peak every time I passed one.

Most people walked by casually, not wishing to give even the slightest impression that they had been inconvenienced by this little fact of life. At night sometimes seven or eight little 600s were aligned like tanks in formation, bobbing up, down, and sideways. People just walked by, talked, and laughed as if naked women were not within five feet of them.

Whenever I passed by, however, I tried to look at these tinny love chambers while appearing to not look. How I imagined the fleshy breasts and legs of the beautiful women inside, just behind the cardboard! How I longed to peek at a pair of buttocks pressed against the window or pushed against the dashboard.

One afternoon I was walking home with my daily ice cream just when a very spirited, romantic liaison was taking place in a car right at the side of the street. I thought that maybe it would be my lucky day; perhaps a small crack between pieces of cardboard would give me a fleeting glimpse of what was going on inside.

I noticed a man whom I had seen around town in various places standing near the front of the car, urging me to come closer. Once I had seen him in the Piazza Municipio with pigeons all over his body encouraging tourists to take a picture of himself. Another time he was charging 50 lire to peek into a cage with a deformed cat in it.

Now he pointed to the car and said, "Come on, have a look inside." I thought there was nothing wrong with doing this, since I had just received an official invitation. My heart was beating fast and I wanted to look, but I had very little money, less than 100 lire, and I thought, "This will not be enough; the man will get mad at me and start a scene, and everyone will run over to see me in front of the "love car."

I walked by, fumbling in my pockets, hoping to feel more change than I thought I had, but I was out of luck. For the next few days I imagined what I might have seen and thought how unlucky I was not to have had more money. At the same time, I tried to convince myself that not having enough money had been the only thing holding me back. During the next few weeks I made sure to have a 100-lire coin with me when I passed that block.

I never saw a "love car" there again, and never saw the same man either. And, to my deep disappointment, I never saw even a small crack between the cardboard pasted on the windows.

—w—

When I returned to Naples every few years for short periods of time, I would recall the people I knew who seemed to be an important part of "my" city. But one by one, slowly, they disappeared. Their impact on me, however, remained, and whenever I felt a desire for better circumstances in my life, I would be reminded of how adept they had been at procuring money, and how fortunate I really was.

My brother Richard and myself walking in the courtyard, 1958.

Nonno and Grandma in the courtyard, 1958.

Nonno, my mother, myself, Grandma, my sister, Aunt Ada, Aunt Lietta, and Aunt Adele in the courtyard, 1964.

My mother and myself at the Villa, 1959.

Aunt Ada and myself, 1959.

Peeling grapes, 1958.

Uncle Bruno in his Fiat 600, 1960.

Maria Teresa and myself, 1960.

My father (left) and his brother Sigi, Naples, 1945.

*Pasquale emerging from the "tiny room,"
1967.*

*My mother and
myself on the way to
Capri, 1961.*

*My sister Michele and
myself in the courtyard,
1964*

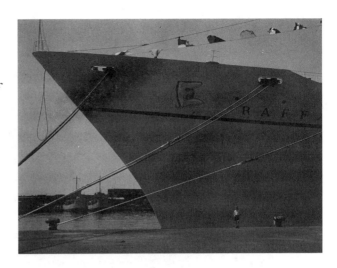

Myself in front of the Raf-faello, *docked in the port of Naples, 1967.*

Myself on the way to Ischia, 1968.

On board the S.S. Vulcania, 1963.

My daughter Micol on the Via Egiziaca, 2004.

The Galleria.

My wife Jayne and myself walk-ing on the Via Egiziaca, 2004.

Fruit store on the Via Egiziaca, 2004.

My wife and myself in the Piazza Plebiscito with the Galleria in the background, 2004.

Myself, my daughter, and my wife in the courtyard, 2004.

Chapter Thirteen

—ᴡ—

Bar Mitzvah in Naples

I was in the midst of receiving bar mitzvah lessons in the Bronx during the spring of 1968. My six-year-old sister was in the room when the rabbi unexpectedly asked her, "Are you American or Jewish?" At first, she was confused by the question, but after some thought, she answered with satisfaction, "I'm English."

That seemed a reasonable compromise. My father is a German Jew, a survivor of World War II. My mother is an Italian Jew, also a war survivor, who moved with her family from Naples to Florence to Perugia and to Rome in order to evade the advancing Nazis.

I, on the other hand, was many things, and I baffled people by not being as accommodating and self-assertive as my "English" sister. I had to convince others that my mother was not a convert to Judaism but had been born a Jew in Italy, much to the dismay of salesmen who tried to ingratiate themselves to the family by turning on the charm in Yiddish—a language my parents neither understood nor spoke.

The rabbi was hunched over and wore a long black coat and a long white beard. His eyes were older than dust. He had been wandering my Bronx neighborhood looking for business when, one day, he showed up at our house. Before I could complain, I was taking Hebrew lessons instead of shooting my beloved hoops.

The rabbi would leave our house once a week with three dollars in his pocket and a slice of Entenmann's walnut ring under his arm. "You're not listening, Robbie," he would sigh, and I usually wasn't. The three months of lessons were interminable for a boy my age. I had a vague notion that these lessons were important, but the notion did not come from me but rather from the disquieting attitude of others who projected their anxieties onto me.

"If you don't have a bar mitzvah, you are not a real Jew," was the unspoken rebuke by well-meaning relatives. So I accepted the inevitable, buckled down to study, and, with relief, one day found that the lessons were done. Finally we were off to Naples for another summer.

Naples was the home my mother had to flee, but it was also the place she returned to when the war was over; the city therefore tugged at me with special meaning.

In 1968 Naples was exuberant because that was the nature of its people, but it was still largely isolated even from the rest of Italy. As an American, I was always a phenomenon on my grandmother's street, where laundry hung on lines suspended between buildings, and men sat on stoops and wicker chairs in aimless contemplation. I heard of anti-Semitic incidents here and there, but my being Jewish didn't seem to matter to anyone I knew.

This summer of 1968 in Naples, I had more lessons to learn for my bar mitzvah, so every day I walked a narrow, cracked concrete path, which was adorned on both sides by bushes and yellow and red flowers, from my grandmother's house to the lower part of the city. There I would arrive at the only synagogue in the city, which also happened to be the "new" rabbi's house.

The Italian rabbi was a character—he would, without fail, greet me in his underwear. He was in his early thirties, enthusiastic, and when I arrived, he would dart briefly in different directions with the purposeful energy that often accompanies thin people.

Each time, upon seeing me, he would say that he hadn't realized it was so late already. Would I mind waiting? He would have his mother get me a drink while he got dressed. Unfailingly I would agree, and down the hallway he would go, bearded and half-naked, to his room.

Meanwhile, down another hallway, the heavy maroon curtain to the synagogue would be opened a crack, allowing a small, diagonal strip of dancing dust to play in a shaft of light. I would be given a drink, usually a Coke, presented on a silver tray engraved in Hebrew letters, and I would sip it respectfully, given that I was in a house of worship.

The rabbi's mother, a frail woman curved as the letter "C," would wait for me to place the empty glass back on the tray and disappeared into the kitchen, returning only to sit down and stare ahead at her dark and heavy furniture. It felt to me that she had been sitting patiently since the time of Moses.

The synagogue evoked in me a feeling of authentic Jewishness, one I had never known before. It was a feeling that spoke from the old walls of centuries of suffering and oppression. The stones of these walls had seen decades of wars and history. For decades Jews had walked through the dark hallway attached to the rabbi's apartment and laid down their burdens there. I could almost hear the screams of fascists and Nazis.

On the other hand, American synagogues, I thought, had an arbitrary "tinnyness" to them. You would turn into their parking lots off Route 22, walk up a pathway, and look through their too brightly colored "stained glass" windows. The insides usually had the look of a Holiday Inn, with the same bright carpets one might expect at a Las Vegas hotel, paired with the brown plastic and chrome chairs one might see stacked in the corner of the "Embassy Room" at a Sheraton Convention Center. Because of the Holocaust, I had decided, synagogues should not have orange carpets. Orange was too bright a color to suggest the serious historical predicament of Jewish history.

I received my "Italian" Hebrew lessons in a space typical of large Neapolitan apartments—a dining room with high ceilings and white marble floors. When I walked, the sound from the heels of my shoes clicked and echoed throughout the house, adding an appropriate churchlike solemnity.

It is said that God listens to the echoes of voices, not to the voices themselves. The rabbi's feet echoed well too. He wore flip-flops, the kind that hung from strings at kiosks near beaches, where vendors sang for children to buy pails and shovels. In a few weeks the Hebrew symbols, which looked more like little wrought iron sculptures than letters, became coherent, and I knew enough of them to be able to sing my part of the ceremony.

When invitations had to be printed for the big event, a printer was found, a style of card selected, and a simple text in English and Italian written for the printer announcing the occasion. The printer wanted to know what this event was about.

"It's a religious ceremony," I explained briefly.

He was slightly confused but accepted the explanation. A few weeks later the cards were ready to be picked up. Before handing over his beautiful box filled with printed invitations, he announced that he had created something special for us, certain we would be pleased. As this was a unique event, he had embossed a Madonna and child on the cover of each invitation as a bonus—free of charge! I now had 100 bar mitzvah invitations with a Madonna and baby Jesus on each one—a first, I'm certain, for a Jewish boy's entry to manhood.

A new set, Jesus-less, was eventually printed, but I kept the original 100 cards. Occasionally I take them out and look at them, wondering how the guests would have reacted had I sent them as they were.

On the big day, a slow-moving, dignified caravan reminiscent of a funeral cortege drove through the old, cobbled streets of Naples. Pasquale, the wise, folksy caretaker of my Aunt Lietta's building, led the way on his Vespa. He knew this was serious business; this occasion called for a display of the inner gravity that was part of his nature. An appropriately somber expression settled and remained on his face throughout the ceremonies.

Meanwhile "regulars" were already sitting in the synagogue when I arrived. Some were rocking back and forth, human tuning forks to God's music, while others had the familiar "synagogue hunch" and that world-weary stare one can see in any synagogue at any time.

There were an unusual bunch of Jews here, some from Africa, others Neapolitan converts who wanted to follow the "true" religion. They looked out of place with afternoon, Neapolitan beards. It seemed to me that most Neapolitans needed to shave twice a day.

I read my lines robotlike, wishing for time to race past. I heard my voice float from my mouth as if I were outside of my own skin. I wondered if I sounded like other bar mitzvah boys with their too-high voices that did not convey the import of their words.

While I did not understand all that I was reading, that fact did not bother me. Religion, I thought, was not a rational explanation of anything but rather a sentiment, a way of "feeling" the world. The Hebrew words, the old synagogue, the old city of hilly streets outside...I took dominion of these images until they became part of the dance of memories that skims on the surface of conscious thought.

Reading a service in English now seemed like cheating, like sending God a telegram in stunted syntax in order to save money. The true feeling of my Jewishness came from the cultural and historical realities of my parents' lives, made so vivid by being in Naples, the place where they had met. Knowing that they survived the atrocities of war, my living in Europe for long periods of time as a child—at the epicenter of the Holocaust—bore down on me with an immediacy greater than any theological beliefs I could ever envision.

The reception was small, intimate, and bereft of excess. Two waiters set up tables and food at my uncle's house, served, and cleaned up four hours later. The cost: $160.

To some, I was now a man. I didn't feel any closer to God, but because I had some knowledge of what my parents went through during the war, I walked forward with the burden of the past, as if I were walking into a wind.

We left Naples by ship a few weeks later. Once back in the Bronx, I knew I would have more explaining to do about what kind of a Jew I was. This would be my last trip to Italy by sea, and my last long summer visit. Sensing this, I ran to the back of the ship to see the landscape slowly fading, and I listened to the muffled sounds from the port, the city's lungs, expanding and contracting, until Naples took its last breath. That summer, leaving Naples, I had become a different person, having learned of a past that changed my concept of who I really was.

Chapter Fourteen

Where Is Virgil's Tomb?

The people of Naples were very proud of their buildings, museums, and monuments. They spoke with reverence about the history of Naples, while nevertheless complaining about all the problems of the "present." They had to make a living, and often a very difficult one, in the city they lived in, but they "owned" its history.

—⁂—

Lucia had a large head, had a pimple on her nose, and wore dark dresses and heavy shoes. She lived in Il Pallonetto, one street over from the Via Pizzofalcone; it was a loud and busy place with merchants selling fruit, fish, meats, and kitchen utensils in the street. Shirts, pants, and undergarments were stretched on lines between the buildings.

Lucia came often to visit her friend who lived next door to my grandmother, but one day the friend was not home, so Lucia sat on a stoop in the courtyard and called me over.

"Another summer, Roberto, and you are here with your Nonni. What have you done this summer?"

"I'm going to the beach almost every day. Not today. It's too cloudy."

"Tell me. There is much to see in Naples. Have you been to the Palazzo Reale [the Royal Palace]?"

"No. You can go in?"

"And the Duomo?"

"I don't think so," not knowing exactly what it was.

"Ahhhhh," she said, drawing out the exhaling "a" sound in a tone I had become familiar with; it meant, "What a pity this is. You have been missing out on something very important."

"And the Cappella di San Severo?"

"I never heard of it."

"Ahhhhh," again. "A big masterpiece is there. Very big. It must be seen. The veiled Christ is there, Robertino. It is a thing of real beauty," she said with careful emphasis on the word "real."

"I will see all of them," I said, not wanting Lucia to continue a catalogue of sites.

"And of course the tomb of the great Virgilio she managed to slip in as a conclusion to her list of sites. "He is one of the greats, like Dante. The bones of Virgilio protected Naples from foreign invasion for many years."

By the tone of Lucia's voice I could tell that she was speaking of gods or demi-gods. The "geee" sound of Virgilio's name leapt out like hot steam. And when she mentioned Dante, the volume of her voice rose at the first accented syllable more than it did for any other word and the tone rose to a high pitch before trailing off to a barely audible "ehhhh."

"DAN–te," she said again, her eyebrows forming a strained squint before she relaxed her entire brow at the end of the word. "He was the greatest."

That night at dinner I brought up the places that Lucia had mentioned as best as I could remember, and my mother said that yes she would bring me to see these places.

"Where is the tomb of Virgilio?" my mother asked my grandmother casually.

"It's somewhere in Fuorigrotta, but I'm not sure where."

"No, no, no," said Ada. "It's near Mergellina, behind the train station. It's very inconspicuous. Nothing much to see."

"It's not in Rome?" asked Aunt Adele.

"It's in Fuorigrotta. I always thought it was in Fuorigrotta. That's what everyone says," my grandmother said with almost certain conviction.

"No, no," said Ada. "It's behind the station, on a hill. Listen to me. That's where it is."

My mother said, "I thought it was near Pozzuoli, near the Solfatara."

"Did you ever see it?" I asked.

"I think so," said my mother. "I don't know. I think so. I don't remember."

The next day I asked around. The police colonel living below my grandmother looked confused when I asked him.

"Big poet, Virgilio. Very big. One of the greats. Like Dante. Big poet of great excellence. His tomb is near Marechiaro. Do you know the song, Roberto...Quando spunta la luna a Marechiaro..." and he kept on singing for a while. "It's a beautiful Neapolitan song, Roberto."

When I asked my Aunt Lietta where the tomb was, she said, "Well, it is definitely the case that it is somewhere. Exactly where, at this moment, right now, I couldn't tell you."

Pasquale didn't know either, but he took the occasion of my asking to tell me that a tomb is of no importance. It is merely stone. It is the works left behind that are important. "Reading a few lines of the Eneide is better than seeing a hundred tombs. Even the tomb of the great Dante, or Benedetto Croce, or any pope would mean nothing to me."

"But do you have any idea where it might be...Virgil's tomb?" I pursued.

"No idea at all," he said.

"Aunt Ada says it's behind the Mergellina train station."

"Well, I suppose that could be. It's possible, but only possible, not much more of a chance than possible."

I thought that my friend Maria Teresa, who was my age, eleven, might know.

"The tomb of Virgilio? It's somewhere right here in Naples. But who cares? Why do you want to see a tomb?"

The next morning I asked the baker, who also did not know. "Do you think the great Virgilio ate a roll as hot and crispy as this one?" and he held it up and then gave it to me.

Within a few days I was starting to forget all about Virgilio and his tomb until I saw Lucia walking into the courtyard.

Running over to her I asked, "Where is the tomb of Virgilio?"

"It is very worth seeing, Roberto. Exactly, with the greatest of precision, in other words to hit the bull's-eye right on the spot with a totally self-assured, absolute accuracy as to where it is, I can't tell you. But make sure you go there. Well, well worth it."

Many years later when I returned to Naples with my children, I thought that I might take my children to the tomb. I asked my Aunt Ada where it was.

"It's behind the Mergellina train station."

"But where behind?" I asked.

"Way, way behind, somewhere way behind."

We all decided to go walk on the Via Roma instead.

—⚉—

Ferragosto, August 15, celebrates the assumption of the Virgin Mary. It is the day, all over Italy, when nobody works... nobody! Cities are desolate; everyone has gone in montagna or al mare (to the mountains or the sea). Shutters cover all the doors and windows as Naples hibernates.

My Aunt Ada and Uncle Bruno were particularly fascinated by the possibilities that this day offered for the city tourist. On those *ferragosto* days when we were in Naples, Bruno liked to drive through all parts of the city, since there was no traffic indulging in racing through the abandoned roads as if it were a guilty pleasure. How easily we moved from one part of Naples to another; from the port we went to the train station in a matter of minutes, usually an exasperating trip.

Once we stopped by the main post office nel cuore della citta (in the heart of the city). Neanche un cane camminava per la strada. (Not even a dog walked in the street.) The buildings seemed nude, exposed and glowing in the heat. Without people blocking the facades of the buildings, how peeled the concrete was, how inarticulate were the graffiti, and how arbitrary seemed the arrangement of doors, windows, and entranceways.

I had walked through other Italian cities during *ferragosto,* but they were very different. The lack of Neapolitans had left an empty, ghostlike, unrecognizable city. Walking between the buildings felt like walking through the eye sockets of an enormous skull: no flesh, no blood, and no skin. Naples was chaos, unpopulated. Bereft of its people, more than any other place I knew, its buildings were merely the vessels of hollow space.

On *ferragosto* we went to Capri with the crowds. One could get there by aliscafo (hydrofoil; the word sounds Neapolitan although it is not) or slow ferry. We took the slow way on a boat that had seen better days. On the boat, I could sit outside on a wooden bench and smell the salt and watch Capri as it slowly grew more and more distinct.

The first thing we did when we arrived was to find an unoccupied space on the beach no bigger than our towel, by the port. A foot, some fingers, and occasionally a piece of leg, all from strangers, made their way on and off our towel. Turning around involved intricate contortions to avoid others' towels and clothing.

I had a small, rubber dinghy, which I filled with air from my lungs, and up and off I went into the water far from the beach. When a boat went by, the dinghy rose and fell and the waves curled up against the sides and then subsided. On one side was the beach, and from the other I surveyed mountains and the craggy coastline extending from Sorrento to the bend where the buildings of Naples ended and the slope that formed the Vesuvius began.

Neapolitans, I thought, had a way of crowding in on me, of being on my blanket and of invading my thoughts. I saw the faces of bus drivers, bakers, shop owners, barbers, and people sitting on the street, and I heard their voices too echoed in the waves against the dinghy. I remember the exact words I told myself that afternoon facing the open water and the bay of Naples: I will always remember the people of this summer.

—w—

I had heard of the Cappella di San Severo even before it was mentioned to me in Naples. A drawing of some of the artworks inside it appeared in one of the Ripley's Believe It or Not cartoon books I had seen.

Inside the chapel is a statue of Jesus lying down with a veil thrown over him. The veil, of course, is made of the same marble as the entire statue, but the illusion of the body being under a real veil, when observed from a short distance, is eerily believable.

Many Neapolitans knew of the "veiled Christ," spoke reverently of its beauty, but had not seen it, and as with Virgil's tomb, did not exactly know where the chapel was located.

"Bellissimo, a great artwork! It must be seen," said Aunt Lietta's housekeeper.

"Where is it?" I asked.

"In SpaccaNapoli." This was an old part of the city where many beautiful baroque churches and chapels may be found.

"Do you know where in SpaccaNapoli it might be?"

"Well, not exactly, but if you go to that neighborhood you can ask. Everyone knows where it is."

So one day I trekked with my mother to find it. Spacca-Napoli has narrow streets, little artisan shops, lots of noise, and an unsavory reputation. I was excited to be there.

A man was standing in the middle of the street with his suit jacket hanging from his shoulders and his arms out of the sleeves in front of him. He held a cigarette and seemed to be contemplating the cobblestones on the ground. Since we had heard that the chapel was open during "irregular" hours, I walked up to the man and asked him if he thought that the chapel might be open on this day.

"So, so," he said.

I asked if he knew where the chapel was and he said that he didn't think so.

Walking a little farther up the street, we came to a woman sweeping the street in front of her "kitchen gadgets" shop. We asked if she knew where the chapel was.

"Eh, eh, eh," she said, "The chapel…the bellissima Cappella di San Severo…" She seemed to be wasting a little time while she was thinking. "The Chapel…the chapel…I know where it is. I know. Listen to me…it's straight up this road. Straight ahead and it will be on your right. It can't be missed. It's up a while, though."

We were thanking the woman and getting on our way when a thin man in a blue suit, wearing spectacles and holding a leather suitcase, stopped us. He had heard the woman's instructions and stopped us to correct them. He spoke to us but ignored the woman, who was standing very close by. As he spoke, she leaned her head toward us to listen.

"It's not straight. Well, yes, it's straight but at a certain point you must make a right and then it's a while down that way. It's not so close to here. Go straight and ask someone further up the road. Everyone knows where it is."

The woman now was leaning against her broom and looked upset. I thanked the man but not too emphatically so as not to insult the woman. She was very upset, however, walking toward us with the broom held firmly in one hand.

"No, no," she screamed. "Absolutely not to the right. It's straight ahead." She ignored the man and gave me a little smile as if to say, listen to me, I'm telling you right. You can bet on what I'm telling you.

"I've lived on this street for only forty years, that's all," she sang out in a little catchy tune.

I gave them both a little "thank you," turning to each with a little smile. It was best to walk up the road and ask someone else,

The agitated man now turned to the woman very sharply. "You're mad, lady. It's the Cappella di San Severo we are talking about? With the veiled Christ?" he asked, now pointing his hand upward with all his fingers tightly together forming a cone with the point formed by his fingertips. Then he looked at me." Listen, listen…Go straight and then it's to the right. That's it. But if you want to walk around just for fun without finding it, if that's your idea of fun, by all means go straight, do as the lady says."

"It's straight ahead," the woman said, proudly raising her chin slightly upward. "Straight as an arrow. I've lived here my entire life. You think I don't know where the chapel is? Take the word of this man just walking by if you wish. It's no matter to me. Make all the rights you want and have a good day with your 'going rights.'"

I wanted to just leave, and my mother was telling me to move on, but the woman now softened her voice and called me over in a gentler tone, trying a new approach. "I only want you to find it, so I'm telling you straight. You want to see the veiled Jesus, no? So just do as I say."

"This is a neighborhood of crazies," called out the man, who was listening in. *"Everyone's a little drunk in old Napoli,"* he started singing.

Now another woman was walking by and had understood what was going on, so she told me, "Come with me. Come. I'll show you."

In the meantime the spectacled man and the woman, now shaking her broom up and down, were engaged in animated discussion about where the chapel was. As we were about to follow our guide, a young man who had come by on his Vespa and stopped to catch the last words of the argument screamed out, "The veiled Jesus is straight up the road about a kilometer, no right just straight up." The Vespa was tilted sideways, almost falling over; he had his left foot on the ground, and his left hand holding the handlebar while the right hand pointed straight ahead. "Straight, straight," he said, making a little pistol of his hand, holding it up to his eye as if to aim it straight up the road. "Straight, straight. It can't be missed."

It seemed that my presence was irrelevant to the argument, so I shouted out a general thank-you to all three travel consultants and looked around for the "follow me" woman. She had vanished. Finally I said an emphatic "thank you" and, with my mother, walked up the street thinking to ask someone else.

"Go where the lady says, but at a certain point you will have to make a right turn."

"A hundred years I've lived here. Listen to me...straight, straight, straight."

We came upon two policemen. Surely, we thought, they would know.

"Is the Cappella di San Severo open today?" my mother asked.

"Sometimes it's open and sometimes it's closed," said one of the policemen, looking at the other one and then back at us.

"It depends, Signora," said the other one.

We waited for a further explanation but there was none.

"And can you tell us how to get there?"

"It's up the road a little bit and then to the left."

"It's not by any chance straight ahead or to the right, is it?" asked my mother, just to make sure.

"Regardless, it may be closed. But it may be open too, Signora."

When we walked a little farther up the road, a sign signaled us to turn right. The thin man with spectacles and briefcase had been correct.

We finally arrived there, eager after so much anticipation, only to find the door locked. A man sitting on a wicker chair saw how disappointed we were and told us to come back a little later. It would probably be open, he informed us. When we asked him at what time, he told us he thought we should come back. He told us that he didn't know but sometimes it opened in the afternoon if...

"If lunch is over and if the 'state employee' is in a good mood and did not have an argument with his wife or brother-in-law. That's what it has come down to, Signora. No one works for their money these days," he said, and then resumed staring up the street and wiping his forehead as if talking had made him tired.

"Welcome to our Bella Napoli," he continued.

We returned an hour later and the chapel was open. The

man who had complained about no one working for his money was still sitting in his chair. He called out, "You are lucky. He had a quickie two-hour lunch today."

The "state employee" standing outside saw how eager we were to go inside the chapel. He finished a smoke and flung the butt away before leading us into the chapel.

"Isn't it a magnificent work of art? It's a true treasure," he said as he adjusted a light on the side of the statue so we could see better. His voice had no more conviction than boredom allowed. Then, he returned to sit in his ticket collection booth and chewed on a piece of bread.

—⚹—

One morning my mother said that we would see the church of Saint Gennaro. That day I was waiting in the courtyard ready to go when Signora Albano, who lived a few floors up from my grandmother's apartment, came out of the building and saw me dressed in my "not-going-to-the-beach wear."

"Where you going today, Roberto?"

"To see the San Gennaro Church, the Duomo," I said.

"Oh, San Gennaro, San Gennaro," she said in a little sing-song. "Say a prayer for me, Roberto, will you?"

"Yes, I will. Sure," I said, but immediately I was a little worried about what to say.

Nevertheless I forgot all about Signora Albano's request when we started on our way to the Duomo di Napoli, the city's main church, not too far from the Cappella di San Severo in SpaccaNapoli. This is where the relics of Saint Januarius, or "San' Gennaro" are kept. A small pamphlet inside the church explained the story of the church and the patron saint of Naples.

Saint Januarius is said to have been beheaded in 305 A.D. near Naples. Little is known of his martyrdom, but many believe a woman wiped up some of his blood on the spot of his beheading and placed the blood in a phial. His body, along with the phial of blood, was eventually brought to the church in Naples, where it was interred. (The church was built over ancient Roman and Greek roads and walls, which can be seen by climbing down stairs from one of the side chapels.)

It is believed that the saint has performed many miracles for Naples, including keeping Mount Vesuvius from erupting on several occasions. But there is a "miracle" that still occurs. For several days in May, in December, and on the feast of Saint Januarius, September 19, the phial of blood is placed near the head and the congealed blood becomes liquefied and sometimes bubbles. The announcement is made, Il Miracolo e` fatto (the miracle has been done). Those who believe can come and kiss the phial. Apparently, this is visible for all to see.

To believers, it is a miracle. The skeptics point out that the "miracle" has something to do with changing the temperature of the contents, and they note that at about the time that the miracle started to occur—the late fourteenth century—the same thing started to happen to other saints' blood in the area of Naples.

The first time I visited the church, I understood nothing of the saints' story, but the scenes inside and outside the church made a deep impression. By walking down to a crypt, one could see the relics themselves consisting of bones and the phial of blood. Several people were in front of the bones, moaning and praying. Women dressed in black were on their knees, kissing their garments, and pointing them toward the relics, while others held their hands together, eyes closed in prayer. One woman was throwing something invisible in the direction of the bones. And a few young men—which seemed unusual to me—were on their knees praying.

I was quiet, observing the scene and wondering what

these people were praying for. In a moment a disturbing question came to mind. I had not been raised in a very religious family, but I had a cultural and historical awareness of my Jewishness, even at a very young age. Being Jewish meant being descendants of other Jews who had lived through wars, famines, plagues, and better times. They had suffered, triumphed, lived in different countries under kings, emperors, and benefactors; however, I had never thought of myself as having a relationship to a supernatural being.

We celebrated Passover each year and told the story of Moses at the kitchen table. I absorbed the part that made sense to me, and I believed it. Moses lived in Egypt, wandered through the desert, and brought his people to Canaan. The burning bush I didn't understand, and I regarded it as exaggeration.

When I was eight or nine, I was told God was everywhere, had made everything, and was all good. I couldn't understand why God would want to be everywhere, what or who made God, and why God didn't stop all the bad things from happening if He had the power. My faith has evolved little from that point.

In front of me were these people who seemed to really believe. What if they were right and praying to the bones of Saint Januarius could help them? What if God listened to them because they believed? Would God listen to me as well if I believed too? Could I ever believe as these people believed?

What if these people were wrong? What if praying to the bones did nothing and no one listened to their prayers? In that crypt that day, I remember thinking about all these questions.

And then another disturbing thought crossed my mind. I had to say a prayer for Signora Albano. Could I pray for her if I didn't believe myself? Would the prayer be valid? Also I didn't know the rules. Could a Jew pray in a church? And could a Jew pray for a Catholic lady? Was that against the rules? Were there any rules, and if so, who would know them?

I knew that I didn't want to go back home and tell Signora Albano that I didn't pray for her. (What if that would bring her bad luck, I thought.) I also didn't want to lie and tell her I prayed when I didn't, because she might have a way of finding out. I therefore decided to pray as best I could. I closed my eyes and prayed that Mrs. Albano would be healthy and that, please, she should get whatever she wished for.

When we emerged from the church, I thought about the people praying inside and whether they were very different once they were out of the church or just like all the other Neapolitans then. I also thought about my grandparents, uncle, and aunt. Did they feel any pressure as Jews in Naples to pray to San Gennaro? Would San Gennaro protect them as well as he could if it were ever necessary to do so?

Outside of the church, we walked down the many steps to the street, where a man held out what looked like a playing card of San Gennaro and prayed for us. I turned around to see the facade of the church and noticed a man in a dark suit—perhaps in his thirties—standing on the steps alongside a blonde woman. A "bent" man walked up to him and said a few words, and then the young man held out his hand and the bent man kissed his fingers. The young man and the blonde then walked to a black limousine parked in front and to the side of the church

This was a confusing day. Many things that I had seen I did not understand. When we got to the Pizzofalcone, the familiar sights greeted and comforted me. Clothing hung from the clotheslines, baskets were being lowered on ropes for the "afternoon fruit man" to drop in his apricots, and the little boys and girls ran naked through the streets. Giuseppino greeted me as always, and Pasquale gave me a salute when I entered my grandmother's courtyard.

A few days after my visit I saw Signora Albano in the courtyard, and she asked if I had prayed to San Gennaro for her. I said, "Yes, I said a good one for you," a little worried that she might ask what my prayer had been and want to know exactly what I had prayed. To my delight, she simply responded, "Grazie, Robertino. Little Robertino has spoken to San Gennaro."

Returning to the Duomo in later years, I had fewer questions to ask myself than I did that first time. The people prayed in the same manner, and the phial of blood was just as I remembered it, enclosed in its glass as it had been for hundreds of years. The world inside and outside the church seemed less dissimilar than that first time I had visited. I didn't know if this, for me, was a good or a bad thing.

—⚬—

My mother remembers Vesuvius smoking during the war. To some it was an omen and to others a reminder of its notorious history. To me it was simply the backdrop of the "typical view" of Naples seen on postcards and paper placemats in pizza shops. The way it seemed to rise from the ocean and slope gently downward toward the city and also toward Sorrento on the far end of the bay gave it the classical look of a mountain, an unnatural preconceived archetype.

From Naples, it had a clearly defined peak, but from the cities it had buried, Pompeii and Ercolano, the gentle slopes that lead to its summit were not dramatic but seemingly benign. One could think from these near cities that climbing to its top might be the perfect place for a picnic.

When I went to visit Vesuvius for the first time at age nine, the closer I got to the crater the less it looked as if I were on the top of a mountain and the less it looked like the mouth of a volcano—until I got to the rim. When I looked inside, the round rim, the rough-textured, sandy landscape, and the bubbling surface could not have evoked the power and potential danger of a volcano any more clearly. Small groups of people were looking in, taking pictures, and consulting guidebooks. Near us was an elderly man, hunched and holding a walking stick with which he pointed inside the crater's "mouth." He wore a hat made of a paper bag on which the word "GUIDE" was written. He signaled with his stick that I should approach with my family, and we did.

"Buon giorno," he said, and then he started pointing. I didn't know what language he was speaking, but to be polite we stayed by him and looked wherever he pointed. I thought that he was speaking Swedish or maybe Dutch.

"In der crateh ist doo hit esplose de undure eet de muntan."

We followed him around the edge of the crater as more people gathered around to hear his explanations. "Frumde fare seede is to looken vider du hole oof der Napoli."

When we had walked about a quarter of the "circle," there was one last rhetorical flourish indicating the end of the tour; then the "Guide" put out his hand for a tip and everyone who had been listening obliged. My mother approached the man casually and asked in Italian in what language he had been speaking.

"Inglese," he said. He must have seen that I was confused and that I was American too. "No understand tutto?" he asked me.

I just smiled, not knowing what to say.

He turned to my mother and in Italian said, "The English they teach in the schools these days isn't worth crap."

That night, back in Naples, I went to the roof of my grandmother's house, which offered an unobstructed view of the bay, including Vesuvius in the background.

It was a dark gray, moonless night. A few faint whistles of the *vaporetti* could be heard in the distance, and a procession of yellow lights rested on the slope of the mountain. I imagined they were a row of climbers resting for the night beside their lanterns. I thought of Vesuvius, how different it had seemed from far, from close, and now at night. But even more, I thought of the guide who could not speak English, who pointed his walking stick at bubbling lava, and who, like so many in this city, had imposed himself on my memory.

Even though we spent most of the entire summer, in Italy, the family sometimes took trips to the south. There I learned how other Italians who had not seen Naples or who knew it only casually, viewed it and also learned how different people were only a day's drive away.

Chapter Fifteen

—ɯ—

Unforgettable: Three Brief Encounters

VINCENZO

Vincenzo was in his early forties, pink-faced, cheery, and slightly portly. Whenever I saw him, he was wearing a suit. His thin-soled leather shoes looked so small for his frame, that he appeared to be about to tip over. He was a businessman who had some dealings with employees of my aunt, and one summer he took a liking to my family and me. We saw him many times that year, often going out to dinner with him.

Vincenzo talked a great deal, and had a small briefcase from which he would pull out papers, graphs, and letters that he would show us; I did not know what they were about nor did I know what he did, except that apparently he wanted to be a partner in a variety of businesses. He spoke vaguely of being an efficient worker, having many good connections, and being able to make money for his clients who used his methods. Apparently he knew a great many people—none of whom, of course, traveled in my circles.

One night we went to Pozzuoli to "do the pizza thing," to refer to it in the popular fashion. Vincenzo had generously

invited my aunt and me to an outdoor restaurant by the sea.
Here we could smell the salty air and hear the waves splashing against the small, tied-up rowboats docked under the
porch where we were eating.

As we sat down, he pulled out a record of Albano—a popular entertainer of the time—and gave it to me, saying that
he wanted me to hear the beautiful old Neapolitan songs that
were on the album. For the remainder of the dinner I looked
at the song titles and read the lyrics behind the album cover.

Vincenzo then turned his attention to my aunt. "There's
no doubt that these new accounting methods will work miracles for the efficiency of the office. Also I know people all
over Europe who could help set the 'whole ting' up." I could
not hear any names but he named many cities. "In Paris there
is 'so-and-so,' in London lives a good friend of mine..."

Then, out of his briefcase flew an array of papers and
charts. Vincenzo somberly pointed to the first paper with a
pen, carefully tracing the lines of a graph, talking nonstop as
he gesticulated. His face wore a new expression every few
seconds, and the volume of his voice rose and fell, sometimes to a mere whisper. I was careful to cut my pizza with a
knife rather than use my hands, and I scrutinized every word
on the album. All the time, I couldn't wait to get home and
listen to it.

After a while Vincenzo put away all his papers and started
talking to me about soccer, my past interests, my present interests, and my future interests, ending with what I thought
about Naples. When the dinner was over, he said that he
wanted to meet me again and asked if perhaps we could all
go for lunch, or dinner, or perhaps we could go to a museum
together. My aunt said that we would talk about it and perhaps we would.

I almost forgot about him until, after a few weeks, I asked
my aunt if we would see him again that summer. She said

that she was very busy and we probably would not see him. I never did see him again.

However, I loved the Albano record and listened to it endlessly that year in Naples and then back home in New York. The next summer I asked my Aunt Ada about Vincenzo. She said something about his having done something not very nice and she was very disappointed in him, but she didn't want to say any more. I didn't pursue the matter, because I could see how upset my aunt was and didn't want to hear anything bad about Vincenzo.

For my aunt, who recognized other motives at work, the evening had been a letdown. But for me it was another exotic memory of Italy. I have never forgotten Vincenzo's friendly face, our seaside pizza dinner when I saw him for the last time, the Albano record, and listening to the waves splashing up against the side of the boats.

And, of course, I've never forgotten the sound of Vincenzo's incessant, exuberant chatter.

Il Professore

Many people had titles in Naples. There were "doms," and "doctors" and "professors." So when a friend of my mother's came to visit at my grandmother's house and introduced himself as "Professore Caldini," I doubted that he was a real professor, but in fact he was. Although his dark blue, shiny suit, tight white shirt, and red tie were businessmen's gear, his relaxed demeanor and slightly disheveled air spoke more of the professor than of the businessman.

"Il Professore" talked to my mother mostly of family, old times, and common friends. Then he started talking about Naples and his theories about the city. Naples would never come out of its poverty, he declared, because the north would always suck out all it could from her. Whenever the government took an initiative to help the south, the north found a way to divert the money to itself. In addition, ingrained in the Neapolitan consciousness was the idea that working couldn't help one get ahead.

"In Naples one works and works and works and gets nowhere because the wages are so low. It's like drowning and flailing in the water in order to stay afloat. And the Neapolitan does not feel he is part of Italy; hence the 'theater' that is always present in all his doings. It's a defense against not feeling a part of a larger community."

He then predicted that Naples would one day emerge from her poverty and be recognized as one of the great European cities, a distinction she richly deserved.

"So you are optimistic about Naples after all?" my mother asked.

"Well, yes, I am optimistic because Neapolitans are very resourceful and will make the best of any situation. Eventually this must lift the entire city out of its doldrums."

My mother looked pleased, but the professor suddenly had a change of tone.

"On the other hand," he went on, "little changes. A new building goes up and then the project is abandoned. The state gives money to a project and then the money disappears, but this happens only in Naples. Have you seen the tall building at the *stazione* [train station]? It's been abandoned, just left there to rot like an old skeleton, a monument to our failure. You come every year. Do you see anything different? No, nothing of course; don't even bother answering. Everything is the same. The man who sits in his chair doing nothing, he won't even buy himself a new chair. Can things change with this attitude? This is Napoli; what can we do?"

"But have you gone by the *villa* [park]?" she asked. "It's been cleaned up a little. You can now walk there *tranquillo* [tranquilly]."

Unimpressed, he continued, "The crux of the problem is

this: The young people, do they have anything to do, anything to look forward to, anything that guides them? I say no. And it is not with pleasure that I say it. It's our fault too, the professors, the educators, basically the older generation. What do we say to them, how do we prepare them for their lives to come? And yet I'm very optimistic."

What? Now he had switched back to a positive approach. My mother simply listened, taking everything in.

"Our generation," he continued, "emerged from the war. There was a new beginning in the air. We had guides we could look to for inspiration, like the great Neapolitan philosophers Benedetto Croce and, of course, Vico." He then went into a lengthy speech about Benedetto Croce, how he had been a guide in the professor's early education and that his philosophy was uplifting.

Then he changed tone again. "Croce was inspiring, but in the final analysis a 'dead end.'" He paused a few seconds. "Until I found the great Vico," he stated with great conviction. He then went into a long description of what Vico had said. Lots of big words poured out of his mouth that I did not understand. Then he paused again before he said, "Now there is no one to look to, E tutto sta la [and that's laying out the whole thing]." He then finished talking about Naples and commented on the good coffee and how happy he was to see my mother.

After he left, I asked my grandmother, who had been listening to the "lecture," whether Professor Caldini had said that Naples would improve or not.

"I don't really know," she said. "But he is a professor. He talks and talks, but it's hard to understand exactly what he means."

I thought about the many words that Professor Caldini had used, even though I didn't understand a lot of them, and considered how wonderful it would be if I too could become a professor one day.

MariaRosa

The beach was called the *Riva Fiorita* and was near the *Marechiaro* area of Naples. It was away from the city in the opposite direction from Vesuvius. It wasn't your traditional idea of a beach. It had no sand, only sharp, moss-covered rocks on top of which towels could be laid. By finding the right spot on a rock, one could wiggle into a small area that had no sharp edges.

I would get to this beach by taking a small walk from the Via Pizzofalcone and then taking an elevator that descended into a tunnel. From there I would walk to *Mergellina*, where I caught a small boat to the beach.

As soon as the boat arrived at the beach—or rather, the collection of rocks jutting into the bay—everyone would run off, towel in hand, to procure one's preferred rock. Despite the discomfort of the rocks, the water sparkled and the lack of sand left bathers with only the tingle of salt on the skin after getting out of the water. By swimming far from the rocks, I could leave behind the sounds of children and conversation. From there, the noise was but a muffled buzz, like a distant motor, and the entire coast could be seen all the way around the bay, past Vesuvius and the mountains to Sorrento,

One day we went to the *Riva Fiorita* with a woman my mother had known since before the war. She had married a wealthy man who lived, as I heard many times, in a large "palatial" house with a sweeping terrace facing the bay. Her husband was a pezzo grande (a big, important man), although I did not know what he did.

Her daughter, MariaRosa, who was in her early twenties, was also joining us on our jaunt to *Riva Fiorita*. She was shapely, almost plump, but not so much that her skin hung over the tight line of the bottom part of her bikini. Rather, the bikini line only made a pinch of her skin so that it puffed out slightly. She looked "just right," I thought. Her breasts filled out the top of her bikini and pulled it down slightly, and her nipples pushed against the inside of the bikini. MariaRosa's golden hair was neatly spun in braids, and her *zoccoli* (flip-flops) had gold straps with neat dark lines running through the middle of the straps. She and her family looked rich— and they were. I was only twelve, but knew that I had met few families with as much money as this one.

On the ride from *Mergellina*, MariaRosa told us that she had a large boat with several sleeping cabins that had a large motor capable of taking her to Capri and Ischia. She claimed that her boat could go anywhere in the Mediterranean that she wished and that it could go a lot faster than the one we were on.

MariaRosa had been to the *Riva Fiorita* before, she told me, but not in the middle of summer, like "now," when it was so crowded. As the boat approached, she gave me a beach towel and asked me to get off the boat and find her a good *scoglio* (rock) that had little moss and few pointy parts.

I ran to the back of the boat, from where the plank would be extended to the platform so everyone could walk off. I was one of the first to get off the boat. There were plenty of people already on the rocks, but there were still a few good ones left, so I picked out what I thought was a smooth stone not too far from the edge of the water and put down Mari-aRosa's towel.

When everyone else arrived, MariaRosa lay down on the towel and thanked me for picking out a good spot. She stretched out her towel carefully, making sure there were no wrinkles in it as it draped over the humps and nooks of the rock. Then she pulled out a pair of huge, round sunglasses and a tube of tanning lotion. As I watched, she put on the glasses, spread some lotion on her arms and belly, and then lay down with one leg stretched out fully and the other bent, her knee pointing upward.

"The sun is so hot today!" she murmured, shifting on her towel and gazing straight up at the blazing orb.

I jumped straight into the water, swam out a bit, and looked back at MariaRosa. Her white skin seemed to shine in the sun, and I could see that her knee was still reaching toward the sky. I also noticed a few men looking her way. I was proud that I was with such a rich and beautiful person and thought that no one should be looking at her except me, because I had come to the beach with her.

I swam farther out, as I usually did, until the people on the beach were only an indistinct blur. I wondered whether MariaRosa's knee was still up, and whether the men were still looking at her. I visualized her putting on her sunglasses and lotion, and I observed how she seemed to own the rock that her towel had claimed as her own.

When I swam back and was close to the rocks, I could see that MariaRosa was still lying in the same position. I walked over to her and asked her if she was going to swim. She replied that it was a nuisance walking on the rocks. She would go into the water just prior to leaving, thus being able to cool off before the hot trip home. Then MariaRosa sat up and looked around her. "Oh, look at how many people there are here." She regarded me carefully. "Would you do me a favor? Would you ask someone if they could spare a cigarette?"

"Me?" I asked.

"Yes. Someone will give you one. It's nothing, just a cigarette."

I wasn't too sure what to do, but I said that yes, I would get her a cigarette.

"There are some guys behind us sitting on an orange blanket. Don't be obvious, but do you see them? Maybe they'll give you one."

I was happy that she had given me something to do for her. I walked gingerly over to the "guys" she was talking about, careful not to place my foot down on a sharp part of the rocks, and asked if they might have a cigarette. They looked in the direction of MariaRosa, saw that I had come from there, and assuming it was for her.

"Of course," they said, pulling one out of a packet lying on their beach towel. I thanked them and dutifully brought it back to her.

"Grazie," she said casually, putting the cigarette down on her towel. I went over to sit near my mother and MariaRosa's mother, then I looked over toward her daughter to see when she would smoke the cigarette.

Now I wondered if she would send me to get a match, so I waited and kept looking her way. But she didn't pick up the cigarette, and finally I walked over to her and asked her when she was going to smoke.

"I'm not going to smoke," she said.

I was confused. "Then why did you want me to get you a cigarette?"

"*Cosi, per fare lo 'snob.'*" (Just like that, to be a snob.)

I didn't know what to make of what she said, thinking it was just a quirk of people who lived in certain parts of Naples. For the rest of the morning on *Riva Fiorita* I tried hard not to look in the direction of the guys who had given me the cigarette, thinking that they might ask me to come and tell them why she didn't smoke it.

MariaRosa finally did swim shortly before it was time to leave the beach. She dried herself off quickly and we got back on the boat to *Mergellina*. During most of the trip back she stood by a railing, leaning into the wind like a carved figure on the prow of old wooden ships I had seen at the Museum of Natural History.

When we got ashore, a driver was waiting for MariaRosa and her family to take them home. We took the elevator inside the tunnel near *Mergellina* and then walked back to the

Via Pizzofalcone. I thought and hoped that we would see MariaRosa again and that she would invite us to ride on her boat to Capri. I imagined looking out over the side of the boat while MariaRosa lay down on the deck. Maybe I would sleep overnight in the cabin on board and jump in the water right off the boat. I was wrong. I thought about her for several days, hoping that she would call in order to invite us to her house or her boat or even to the beach again. Soon she faded into memory, as if the day I had spent with her had not been real.

Like Vincenzo with his briefcase full of diagrams and charts and Professor Caldini with his contradictory opinions, MariaRosa walked in and out of my life during one of those summer days in Naples and never walked back in again.

Chapter Sixteen

—ແ—

Adventures in Appetites

Rita Pavone's hit song "La Partita di Pallone" was everywhere during the summer of 1964. Her youthful voice could be heard from the jukeboxes in the cafés and blasting from the radios on every beach, "Perché, perché, la domenica mi lasci sempre sola/ Per andare a vedere la partite di Pallone?" (Why do you leave me alone every Sunday to go see the soccer game?), she demanded to know.

This was the summer I began to perfect my foosball skills. By putting a rolled-up sock in each of the goals, my friends and I could retrieve the ball without it going down the hatch, play all day, and save ourselves many hundreds of lire.

My father, as usual, did not join the rest of the family on the ship to Naples that summer. Rather he flew in some time in August, and we all took a car trip with him to Maratea along the coast south of Naples.

Earlier that year my Aunt Ada replaced her Fiat 600—the "little mouse on wheels," as I then thought of it—with her gray Opel Kadett. The 600 (so named for its 600-cubic-centimeter engine) cost about $800 and was the car that put Italy on wheels. It was tiny but reliable, and affordable for most people. "Even a sanitation man can afford a car these days," my Aunt Adele would say.

The 600s zipped through the streets of Naples with abandon, sounding like swarms of bees because of their sewing-machine-size, high-pitched engines. Because there were few roads in Naples, there was little traffic, no traffic lights, and a few driving rules that were ignored by virtually everyone.

We had borrowed Aunt Ada's 600 in previous summers, and it got us to all the small towns we loved to visit in southern Italy. Occasionally, if we chanced upon a steep hill, the poor little engine would give out, requiring me to get out, walk, and then get back in the car when I reached the top.

But now we had the Kadett for our trip. Although it was smaller than a VW Beetle, it was luxurious compared with the Fiat: large, spacious, and comfortable. I fervently hoped that I wouldn't have to get out of it when we came to a steep road.

Because there was no *Autostrada* (highway) in those days, the roads to the little town of Praia a Mare, less than 200 miles away and along the coast, seemed long. They wound their way up and down mountains, crossed canyons, valleys, and many small towns. Within a short time I was reliving the seasickness I had experienced while on the ship.

At lunchtime we would look for a place to stop and eat, but there didn't seem to be any. From the road we could see many *cittadine* (little cities) with small white and gray buildings and brick roofs on the top of mountains. None of these indicated the presence of a restaurant, so we decided to leave the main road. The towns were built hundreds of years ago and were high up and "protected" to fend off invaders from other towns. Each town was built around a large, open area, the main piazza just in front of the town church. Each town extended outward from this central piazza to the farthest buildings, which formed the outlines of the town's limits, each in the shape of a different parabola of varying sizes.

We decided to stop in one such town and made our way up the only road, which brought us to the piazza in the center just in front of the church. A few cars were parked on the outer rim of the piazza, and a few chickens walked in the street. Fortunately, a *salumeria* (delicatessen) was open and we went inside to ask if there was a place where we could have lunch.

"Hah," chuckled the young woman behind the counter, "not in this town."

She then turned to me and asked where I was from. I was surprised she didn't ask my mother or father, but then decided she had chosen me because I was less likely to give her a tricky answer. I didn't know if she meant "from" Italy or "from" another country.

"Da dove? Da dove?" (From where? From where?), she repeated.

I answered that we were from Naples.

"Ha!" she said. "You are not in Naples any longer. In Naples, yes, there are places to eat. Not here."

Just then a young boy walked in. Could he be her brother? He seemed to have emerged from a room just behind the counter, very curious about what was going on.

"These Neapolitans are looking for a place to eat lunch," said the young woman. "I told them there is no place here, but let's see..."

"I can catch one of the nice chickens running around for all of you," the little boy joked.

Then the young woman turned to the little boy and asked, "Is Signora Anna around? Go and check. Go call for her," she commanded, and off ran the little boy.

"I wouldn't mind going to Napoli one day," she said just as the little boy came running back in.

"Yes, she is in!" he announced jubilantly.

"Come follow me," said the woman. My father agreed to

follow her, but first he had a small request. Directing his attention to the boy, he asked, "Would there happen to be a restroom somewhere?"

"Atto piccolo o atto grande?" (The "little thing" or the "big thing?), the boy asked without any hesitation.

"The little," said my father, immediately understanding his meaning.

"Then follow me, signore," he said, walking my father behind the counter. The boy opened the door that he had previously emerged from and indicated that this was the desired bathroom.

We then followed the woman to meet "Anna," hoping that she owned a small *trattoria* where we might eat. But there was no *trattoria.* Instead the young woman knocked on the door of a house on the street and a middle-aged, smiling woman appeared.

"Si, si, possono mangiare qua" (Yes, yes, they can eat here), she agreed.

"We weren't too sure what to do, but we walked into the house and were escorted to the dining room, where we sat down. Anna asked us to wait a moment, and the woman who had brought us left, telling us that Anna was an excellent cook and that she would prepare a whole meal for us. My father looked slightly uncomfortable, my two-year-old sister crawled about the room, and I secretly hoped that the woman would not make any cannelloni with cheese, which I detested.

Then Anna disappeared, and we heard her voice calling from another room. "So you are from Naples? How nice. Well, I suppose Naples is a place like any other, or am I wrong?"

She didn't wait for an answer but kept on talking. "I suppose it's quite a ride to Naples. A nephew of mine lives there. He went there to work. What can he do here? Look after the chickens? It's a few hours from here by the auto, isn't it?

Yes, there is a bus from here. I hope you don't think we are nowhere. There's a bus from here that goes everywhere. Still, Naples must be worth seeing, I'm sure. My mother brought me there as a little girl. I remember the sea...beautiful... beautiful. Okay, signori, come in and look at the table."

When we went in, we were greeted by a beautiful table set with silverware, three glasses at each setting, and em- broidered linen napkins.

"Oh, I hope we have not put you to so much trouble," said my mother.

"Of course not!" Anna replied easily. "What is it, a table setting for lunch? Niente, niente, niente, signora. And what might you all desire to eat today?" she requested, as if we were sitting in a restaurant and she was taking our order. "Were you thinking along the lines of fish or meat of some kind? Of course the pasta will be the first dish, along with vegetables and fruit, of course. But we can make the pasta with some little thing in it, maybe some zucchini or maybe just plain. How would you like it?"

Still unbelieving that we were about to get our fond- est wish for dinner, I said that I would like veal cutlets and fried zucchini, and was going to add more before my mother pushed me.

"We certainly don't want you to go to any trouble, signora. Whatever is fastest and easiest for you," my mother said gratefully, shooting me a look.

"Nothing to worry about, nothing at all. Let me cook up a few different things and then we can eat. And of course some wine. We'll call it 'the house wine,'" she laughed, "although it's not really from this particular house."

When she left the room, my father looked at my mother and said, "We're going to be here all day!"

"O, mamma mia," chimed in my mother. "Who has made us do this? Look at this table. What can we do?"

"Sit, sit, sit. Make yourselves at home," said Anna, returning from the other room.

We sat down and Anna disappeared again. We were all whispering under our breaths about what this all would mean, when we would eat, that we didn't have so much time to spare. Most of all, we wondered how much all of this special attention was going to cost!

After a few minutes Anna appeared in finer clothing, holding her pocketbook. She walked to the door and said, "I won't be too long. Make yourselves comfortable." And she was out the door.

I think everyone was stunned except my sister, who happily crawled under the table.

"What in God's name have we done?" my father cried, now despairing of any escape.

"O, mamma mia, where is she going?" asked my mother, knowing the answer. Anna was clearly going out to get our dinner.

I looked more closely at the dishes and declared them quite fancy. "They're a little like Aunt Lietta's," I pointed out.

My father's mind was on other matters. "She's going to have a cow slaughtered. I just hope we don't have to wait until the meat is aged too."

My father was getting worried about how far we could drive after lunch and was thinking that we might have to stop sooner than planned. My mother was saying how much she would like to get out of the whole situation but that now, with Anna having set up the table and buying the food, it was impossible. I was wondering whether the woman had taken me at my word about the veal cutlets or whether my mother's nudge had nullified my request. I was hoping that if she did, she would buy the good tender kind of veal, the young veal, not the *vitellone*—the tough kind.

We thought we were alone in the house until we saw a little girl come into the dining room. She told us that mamma had gone to buy the food and asked if we might want anything to drink in the meantime. She then went into the kitchen and started cleaning up while we continued to sit at the table.

It was about an hour before the woman came back with two full bags of groceries. "And here I am," she said. "See, no big deal. I had to call the butcher from his house, but here we are, all ready, all ready to cook. See, no big deal. Ecco mi qua, ecco mi qua." (Here I am. Here I am).

My father was no longer irritated but rather amused. "Oy, vey," he said.

Anna went to the kitchen with the bags, and soon we heard a chorus of crumpling paper, heavy thuds of wrapped food hitting the counter, and clinking bottles. Meanwhile we became hungrier and hungrier. My mother said that she had surpassed the word "hunger," while my sister was getting cranky under the table. I was still focused on young veal versus the *vitellone*.

After about half an hour, finally, Anna carried in a big bowl of pasta burgeoning with fresh tomatoes, zucchini, and eggplant. As we dug into our first course, Anna resumed her work in the kitchen and soon brought out the "seconds," a plate of thinly sliced roast beef layered to look like a fan, a whole fish with the head on the side of the dish as a decoration, and veal cutlets—the good, young kind. Of course, cheese and fruit and a little espresso followed to top things off. We all looked at each other approvingly, satisfied at the delicious meal.

It was now several hours since we had walked into Anna's house and we were as well satiated as lions after zebra kill. We thanked Anna profusely and told her what a good meal she had prepared and said that we would be on our way now and not forget her wonderful food and hospitality. How much did we owe her? my father asked.

She then walked over to him with a piece of paper on which the price was written down. I didn't look at him when he first looked at the paper, but I just saw him taking out a few bills from his pocket and giving them to Anna and then thanking her again.

No one mentioned the cost, although even I was curious. We talked about the whole adventure for the next hour, and my father finally said, "And it wasn't expensive! Think of what that woman did."

"Maybe we will stop on the way back…if we have an extra day to spare."

The rest of the ride to Praia a Mare was mostly nauseating. The Kadett wound its way through the one-lane roads up and down the mountains, and we had to go slowly, following the large trucks, behind which we formed part of a "tail" of cars.

We went off the road into one of the towns so I could get out of the car and walk around to rid myself of the nausea. No one was to be seen in the heat of early evening except a man who was sitting on a wicker chair looking as if he had been on it for decades. I approached him to ask how the road from this town to Praia a Mare was.

"Is it straight?" I asked, hoping that the question would somehow change what I knew to be the reality.

"All the way to Salerno, oh, it's very straight, all right," he said to my amazement and joy. But as I turned and walked away, he added, "… as straight as a snake."

The bends in the roads were worse than the bends in a snake, and it was getting hot too. I could feel the wet sweat bathing my whole body.

We arrived in Praia a Mare late that night, checked into a small, hot hotel that boasted a "cool air box" to little effect. We then went out to the local café, where Rita Pavone's voice drifted out of the nearby jukebox. We sat down at a table, but no one came over to take our order. A waiter walked back and forth bringing espressos to people at other tables but did not ask us anything. After a while my father stopped the waiter and asked him if he had Coke. The waiter replied, "Yes" and then disappeared for a while. When he reappeared, he did not have a Coke with him, so my father then stopped him again, asking a bit more impatiently, "You have Coke?"

"Yes," the waiter said again.

"Well, then, may I have one?" my father asked.

"Oh, sure," he said, and brought it out.

"I like the pace of this place," said my father.

It was a relief to him and all of us after Anna's meal; even though she had prepared unexpectedly delicious food, we felt that we had been captives to her hospitality. Now no one bothered to serve us even when we wanted to be served.

—⟁—

The next morning we were on the beach. The sun burned on the coarse sand pebbles and twinkled off the peaks of waves. The water was blue, clear, and silvery. I was used to crowds on the beaches near Naples, but there were only a few people here.

The concierge at the hotel told us that on weekends there are a few more people. "Even some people from Napoli are making their way here," he told us.

That weekend there were two or three more families than usual. "Did you see the *Svedese*?" the concierge asked. "There's a beautiful blonde woman from Sweden who is in town. She's some kind of a star in Sweden, and she's here on vacation. You will see her, and you will know her when you do. She's not from Napoli, I can assure you of that."

The next day we saw her. She was a twenty-ish, tall, blonde

woman sitting alone on her large, colorful towel. Her long hair swayed to the side as she turned, and her thin body and legs stretched when she lay down. She gave a quick wave in our direction to acknowledge us as her little fingers danced up and down. A few, small wet pebbles stuck to her thigh.

There was a lot of talk about the *Svedese* all through the town. The concierge of the hotel asked if we had finally seen her; the waiter at the café who would not bring a Coke until asked specifically to do so asked us if we had seen the *Svedese,* and the *salumiere* (deli man) asked us if we had seen her as well.

"Every day she comes in here to buy something at about 4:00 P.M. If you like, you may also hang around. It's my invitation," the deli man announced to us.

That afternoon I was at the café getting an ice cream and the *Svedese* walked into the piazza. A few men who had been standing around were staring at her and nodding to each other in approval. The waiter came out of the café, leaned against the wall, and started staring as well.

"And so the *Svedese* is going for her daily walk," he said.

She walked over to the café and sat close to us, giving us a nod since she had recognized us from the beach. I was eating my ice cream when I noticed that men were coming out of their homes, walking up the street and leaning against the wall on the outer edge of the piazza. It was starting to get crowded in the little piazza. Word had obviously gotten out that the *Svedese* was having her espresso. Then men started walking by in small groups and saying hello to her. When one group walked by, another began its trek to say hello.

"But look at this," my mother said, a little uncomfortably.

I was very involved in my Cornetto Algida ice cream and didn't think much of the little crowds coming by, and the *Svedese* didn't seem much concerned at all. She nodded at each group of men that walked by and smiled. After she got up to leave, she hadn't walked too far when she had to adjust a strap on her sandal. A few of the men moved in very close around her and watched her as she put her foot up on a bench to make the adjustment. The men leaned in a little to get a better look, and one asked her if she needed any help. He was willing, he told her, if she so desired. She simply smiled and then moved on.

The small crowd that had gathered to watch her adjust her strap now walked a few paces behind her, and the rest of the men, leaning against the buildings and still standing in their groups, began to break up and walk their separate ways. Within a minute the crowded piazza was mostly empty again as if the men had been flies on a piece of bread and someone had sprayed the bread with DDT.

We continued to see the *Svedese* on the beach the next few mornings. Then it was time to go back to Naples. When we were checking out, the concierge of the hotel asked us where we were from.

"From Napoli," I yelled out.

"I've been to Napoli," he said to us triumphantly.

I remember as we were leaving in the Kadett how strange it seemed that we had driven down to Praia a Mare in one day and that so few people had been to Naples, and when they had it was such a big to-do. And also it seemed unusual that so few Neapolitans were at this beach in the middle of the summer. I thought of myself as quite a traveler for simply having come from Naples, let alone America.

On the way back home we talked a lot about Anna's meal, the waiter who would not bring a Coke, and the *Svedese*. The town we stopped in on the way to Praia a Mare we called "Anna's town," the café where we went every day we called "The café where they don't bring you a Coke," the beach we called "the beach of the *Svedese*," and the piazza we called "the place of the staring men."

Chapter Seventeen

—⚊—

Ships, a Walkway, and a Train

SHIPS

Between 1955 and 1969 I made twenty-six transatlantic crossings by ship between New York and Naples. "Pack up your bags," my father would tell us "We're leaving tomorrow." That's how we would hear about going to Italy for another summer. Since my father was a travel agent, he received cabin space only at the last minute if a cabin became available. We always went first class, mingling sometimes uncomfortably with the famous and the powerful as well as with other travel agents and their families who might be aboard.

Upon knowing which ship we were to sail on, I would learn about all its important specifications until my knowledge became encyclopedic—as well as highly annoying to those around me. Very few of my friends and relatives were interested in knowing which ship had "Denny Brown Stabilizers."

Many of the ships we traveled on were of the Italian line "Societè Italiana di Navigazione," whose brochures championed the "sunny southern route." These included the *Satur-*

nia and *Vulcania*, 23,000-ton ships built in the 1920s. These were the "old tubs" of the fleet but were nevertheless arrayed in opulent décor.

Most memorable was the large central stairway that opened up into the main lounge much like that in the *Titanic*. The improvised movie theater consisted of a large sheet tied between two pillars in the main lounge and a 16mm projector placed strategically on a table. My brother Richard and I were often pressed into service, as people were needed to hold up the sheet while it was being tied.

One of the most impressive ships I traveled on was the majestic 81,237-ton Queen Mary, where our suite was large enough for me to play touch football. I also had a private butler, who nightly wanted to know when "Master Zweig would like to have his shoes shined." Every dinner menu had the date embossed on it with my name, "Master Robert Zweig."

I remember approaching the ship as a five-year-old. It was anchored at sea in Southampton, England. We took a small boat out to it in a thick fog, and it came into focus at the last instant, when we were nearly upon it. I could not see the top, the front or the back of the ship, only a small part on either side of the door we entered.

Sitting comfortably in the liner's dining room or lying down in the cabin, I had little sense of movement or gain. Most days passed in routine fashion, with meals and other events spaced out in much the same manner. Entertainment consisted mostly of bands and singers, sometimes made up from the crew. I spent hours playing Ping-Pong and winning many tournaments. Each successive day, however, was better, since it was one step closer to the final destination.

The voyage took between seven and twelve days, depending on where it stopped. Typically the ship docking in Gibraltar, the first land to be seen after the Atlantic crossing. This was an especially exciting stop, because it signaled that we would finally be in the Mediterranean and within two days of Naples. In Gibraltar I looked forward to seeing its unique monkeys and a view of the African coast.

There was no port to dock in at Gibraltar, so the ship stopped close to the island. Moroccan traders would come alongside and scream out about their wares, usually colorful dishes and small statues and toys. They would throw up a rope that curled around the ship's railings and send up the items by pulling the rope. After inspecting a desired item, you could scream at them, bartering for a better price.

Then on to Barcelona, with its wavy, curved Gaudi buildings that looked as if they were melting. Next was Genoa, a well-run Italian city that my Neapolitan family referred to as "refreshingly un-Neapolitan" because its infrastructure functioned normally.

On one trip we walked off the ship in Lisbon and were greeted by the same taxi driver we had hired the year before. He seemed, surprisingly, to be genuinely excited to see us and took us on a long city tour, all the time talking about his children. He gave us his address and phone number and told us to call him if we were ever in port again. A few months later we sent him a box of clothing for his children along with some other items. He wrote back that his children said the box "was sent by God."

However exciting these stops, they were only a prelude to the main event—arriving in Naples, my "other" home.

Nights at sea thrilled and scared me. On moonlit nights a glimmering white carpet would begin at the horizon and end where it pushed against the side of the ship. As the ship moved, so too did this carpet of light.

But on dark nights either the horizon was not seen or the demarcation of sky and water was marked by only a slight gradation of black. On such nights, as I glanced toward eternity, an anxious longing, without object or cause, would sit upon the silence. With my chin resting on a wooden railing and the pungent aroma of salt in the air, I imagined myself a lonely traveler on the ocean, floating aimlessly, urging the horizon to greater distances. At sea it is easy to believe that there is no end to the ocean and that the ship will move in beatific monotony forever.

I do remember a more intense feeling one night. I was leaning out over the railing of the *Vulcania* enveloped in darkness. The loneliness of endless space and time came upon me as the waves hit the boat in tedious succession. I suddenly thought that this was a glimpse of what it would be like to be dead. It had never occurred to me before that death was eternal and that my life was but a flare of light that shone brightly for a moment, then extinguished itself. Because my parents had lived "another life" before the one I knew in New York and it had seemed so long ago, their history was my anchor to the past. The past had seemed deep and far and remote. But on that night it seemed impotent, fragile, and very close.

Looking back, I trace many joys and fears to my sea voyages. And I dream constantly of being on a ship and looking out over dark, rough water.

The last trip I made by sea to Naples was in 1968. By that time the era of transatlantic ship travel was coming to a close. Within a few years there would be no more liners sailing between New York and Naples. Many of the great ships were sold for scrap metal, or simply docked, looted, or burned.

I came to see these ships—and all ships—as objects of true beauty. They were built to be small, self-enclosed utopias. Their portholes, wooden decks, and suspended lifeboats on outer decks suggested movement and an outer world, but their insides spoke of protection, wealth, and isolation from everyday concerns.

I invite the reader to visit a port city and find an ocean liner at the dock. Then regard it closely from the front, observing the curve of its bow, a testimony to ambition and determination. They are machines well suited to their purpose—built in accord with nature's laws, yet seeming to defy them. They are able to glide through endless seawater with illusory ease.

And, like dreams that bridge the night to the morning, those magical voyages were like interludes between vastly different worlds.

A WALKWAY

A narrow, cracked, concrete path, adorned on both sides by bushes and red and yellow flowers, snaked its way from the hill on which my grandmother lived to a lower part of the city. I took this walkway every day while staying with my grandmother; it led me down the hill to my bar mitzvah lessons in the local, one-room synagogue. Because I had wanted my Italian relatives to be at my bar mitzvah, I had it in Naples.

Naples, a city of hills, has many such pathways, and I prided myself on being, at the tender age of thirteen, a savant of the city's hideaways and back streets. This particular path had few travelers each morning, giving anyone traversing it the mistaken sense that—but for the sounds of distant traffic and boat whistles—Naples was a small, sleepy town somewhere on the outskirts of a large Italian city.

My mind, however, was often less on the scenery and more on my upcoming Hebrew lesson. I was focusing on the peculiar shape of the Hebrew letters that looked more like miniature wrought iron sculptures than letters, and on the demanding "Rabbino" himself. I was feeling quite resentful at having to study when, at that very moment, one of my friends was probably jumping in the water at the nearby Sea Garden beach in Mergellina.

The wall of the alleyway that led to my lessons was lined on one side with windows and doors. At one of the windows, about halfway down to the rabbi's house, sat an elderly, white-haired woman who looked out over the traffic passing her house. Her gaze was deliberate, eyeing the walkers who passed her window with suspicion. She owned the little piece of walkway in front of her house and, as a landowner, felt it her right to charge for the use of her property.

She found the exact amount to charge to be a rather perplexing question, for the smallest denomination coin (5 lire or ¾ cents) was apparently too much, and she didn't want to give incentives to walkers to find alternate routes to their destinations.

Cleverly, the woman found a satisfying way to handle this dilemma. She charged 3 lire. Upon giving her a 5-lire coin—about as heavy as half a small feather—I would receive back two pieces of paper, each of which had "1 lire" written on it. It is generally known that long ago banks had printed their own money. Now, in Naples in 1968, there was a woman in an alleyway leading to the rabbi's house who was distributing her own version of "legal tender."

Since the two pieces of paper were not enough to secure "safe" passage back up the alley, another 5-lire coin would have to be collected on the return walk. This would leave four pieces of a "1 lire" paper that would be good for one passage with one remaining piece of paper. An extra round-trip passage was therefore necessary to secure one's money's worth.

Thus two round-trip passages plus one other voyage would be the most efficient use of real money and the pieces of paper she dispensed. The old woman had figured out that taking five one-way trips was very unlikely and that some unsuspecting pedestrians would be left with a few pieces of her paper without having any use for them. Even at that time, I remember thinking how ingenious her practice was. Yet it was typical in Naples, a city where resourceful ways of making money were common.

Almost every day the summer of my bar mitzvah, I walked back and forth on the little path, counting how many lizards I could see on each trip, thinking of the Hebrew letters, conjuring up possibly disastrous scenarios for the bar mitzvah, and collecting the woman's little pieces of paper with due diligence. I would place three of them in her hand, happy in the knowledge that on some particular day I did not have to pull out a whole 5-lire piece.

The "little Jewish street," as I came to think of it, became my refuge from the noise and commotion of the busily trafficked roads, and the 3 lire toll collector became the gatekeeper of my peaceful walks. How easily I slipped into the dreams that the little street infused in me. Walking peacefully on its cobblestones became the perfect prelude to my Hebrew lessons with their sonorous, incomprehensible prayers that echoed in the synagogue.

Then one day everything changed. The shutters of the woman's house were closed and locked. Ahead of me I saw a man coming along the path, stop, and linger by her window, unsure of what to do. For a moment or two he held her pieces of paper in the air, unsure of how to unburden himself of them. Then, his decision made, he resumed his stride as we awkwardly passed each other in front of her house. While no words were spoken, I glimpsed relief, then unease in the face of my fellow traveler. The old woman's absence was a change in our routine, true. But even more unsettling, her locked shutters seemed to imply our greater vulnerability to the outside world. It was as if the chaos of the city had been given permission to enter this protective place, where it now hovered ever more closely around us.

A TRAIN

As my train sped along the tracks between Rome and Naples one summer in 1974, I thought of Naples in years past with a longing for my lost youth. This was the first trip I was making after the many years of consecutive summers with my grandparents. Now, although I was only nineteen, the horizon had moved a bit closer, and the distant mountains I saw from the train window were reminders of perpetuity amid flux. The lulling ta-ta-tum ta-ta-tum of the train set a rhythm for my thoughts.

My arrival by train did not offer the drama that I had always experienced when arriving by ship. The ship's slow entrance into the harbor had filled me with expectancy until our arrival was confirmed by seeing my Nonno Max in his straw hat, cigarette in hand, waiting by the dock.

The Bay of Naples forms a semicircle, welcoming ships into its arms. As we unhurriedly slid silently into the port, the small islands of the bay became visible, and finally Vesuvius formed the backdrop to the whole scene for the final moments before docking. On most summer days the scene was drenched in sunlit clarity.

By contrast, the train was now whirring past dilapidated yellow plaster walls with dried branches hanging out of them. And abruptly I found that we were approaching the station. I began to wonder which had altered more drastically, Naples or me.

Sitting opposite me were two boys, twins, along with their mother, and also a woman who was accompanying me on this trip, with whom I had fallen in love. As trees, telephone poles, and fields blurred in the background, her face was a portrait of serenity staring into blank space. Only a slight movement of her neck revealed that she was breathing. The twins were fighting for space; their mother was pushing and pulling to even out the margin of seat between them, and the intermittent light and shadow cast from the window played upon their faces. I had wanted to put my hand on my beloved's thigh and feel the electric jolt of love, but I did not.

In previous years such train rides had been the scene of intimate conversations. Unlike the curious and easily distracted child that I had been, most train passengers in the early 1960s in Italy were not tourists. They were businesspeople or young men and women from the north going to visit "Mama." Most of them bore the tuned-out stares seen on people's faces in public lounges or waiting rooms. Sometimes, however, one Buon giorno could lead to the most confidential information, the kind given only to strangers. I had learned of infidelity and suicide attempts and troubled relationships. One woman had told me of her "little Giorgio," a boy much like me who was sick and wouldn't eat. She was going to see him in the hospital in Naples.

A young man once told me of his army service, how difficult it had been to be away from his mamma's cooking. By the time the destination had been reached and the passengers had gotten off, I knew more about their intimate secrets than I knew of those of my own close friends. My new confidants had left the train cleansed of their angst and satisfied that they had unburdened themselves to a boy whom they would likely never see again.

On this trip, however, I was happy to look away from others' lives and into my own. The interruption of five years since my last visit had coated my usual sense of strong familiarity with Italy with a thin varnish of indifference. I was finding it a little harder to assimilate into the language and the requisite dramatic hand gestures.

When I was a child, the ten-month interludes between vacations had seemed endless, but once I arrived in Naples, within a day or two I was speaking a kind of "Bronx-Neapolitan" and running around the neighborhood like a kid from the Palonetto—one of the livelier city streets. Now, sitting on this train, I feared I might not have that feeling of totally belonging, of being just like any other Napoletano.

As we approached Naples, I wrote "I Love You" on a piece of paper and gave it to my inamorata. She looked at it a long time, smiled, put it in her pocket, and resumed staring out the window. The train was slowing and familiar sights could be seen, blurred in the distance. Soon we would be on the platform, walking out of the station and back on the streets I had known so well. I wanted desperately for her to feel the city's pulse and rhythm as I had. Still, her presence tugged at me, pulling me away from Naples and the past and toward my future.

My grandparents were no longer alive, so I would not stay in their house, the one I had lived in and played in every summer of my youth. My childhood was over, and the brilliance of every moment, magnified by auras of joy and despair, had been replaced by a more dispassionate perspective. Being in love only punctuated my distance from the days of my youth.

During this journey I would travel and experience the city in a new way, trying to impress its wonders on another's eyes. Would she see it the way I did? Would I see it the way I had?

When we got off the train at Mergellina—a station on the outskirts of downtown Naples, but closer to my relatives' house—the familiar sounds of high-pitched honking horns and the conversations in Neapolitan momentarily immersed me in the magical aura of my youth. These sounds and sights had been receding over the past years but were brought back in a rush. Still, because I was now nineteen, or because of the passage of years, a small feeling of separation from my former self lingered. In the following days, my future wife and I traversed many pathways of my former life. Everything looked the same, but I did not feel the same.

One night we strolled along the Via Caraciolo, the street hugging the bay that gently curves along the water's edge. The moon shone smooth and white like a polished gem, and the waves exhausted themselves on the rocks along the shoreline. As we sat on a bench, I saw the gleam of moonbeams glittering in her eye, and I thought of how different Naples would be from this day on.

Chapter Eighteen

— ∞ —

Return to Naples

In the summer of 2004, while traveling to Naples with my family, I found myself standing in the middle of that courtyard of grandmother's that, as a boy in the 1960s, I had once claimed as my domain. I had fantasized for many years about this return to childhood. I had imagined entering the courtyard in endless variations, and envisioned startled ghosts, shaken by my appearance. But when I discovered the big door unexpectedly open, allowing me to step straight into the rectangular courtyard, I found myself simply, uneventfully there. That summer I was forty-nine years old. This trip was very different from my previous visit ten years earlier, for at a certain age your past casts a longer shadow. I must have looked confused, because a woman, a little younger than me, yelled from her balcony, "Are you looking for something?"

I told her that my grandparents had lived here many years ago, that I had stayed here every summer in the 1960s, and that I was just looking around. "They were the Calabis," I said. "Recanati was my aunt. She owned the building."

"Yes, yes," she said, "I remember them a little bit. Where are you from?"

"I'm American. I'm here on vacation."

I had last seen Aunt Lietta twenty-seven years before. She was nearly 100 then; I remember seeing the outlines of her bones underneath her blanket. As I spoke to the woman on the terrace, I was looking at Aunt Lietta's ground-level kitchen window, newly painted. I had climbed through this window into the unearthly world that was inside; now I would not have wanted to look inside, fearing that I might see just an ordinary kitchen.

A rectangular, marble walkway 6 by 40 feet led to the door of my grandmother's house. Here chairs had been assembled at four o'clock every afternoon to usher in the end of the siesta for everyone except me, for whom taking out the folding chairs signaled the end of afternoon listlessness. I remember looking up at the window where my grandmother sat, hip broken, in her eternal, sad-eyed pose.

I recalled the spirited housekeeper, Maria, who believed in almost nothing new. Could there still be a person living here now who could be as skeptical of the modern world as she was?

"Don't ever go in the flying gizmo. It's too dangerous," she would scream out. "They're all going to fall." Nor did she believe in the Jolly Green Giant, because when I told her that we had frozen vegetables in New York, she gave no credulity to the "nonsense" I was imparting on her.

She would scream out spontaneously in a musical voice, "Robertino, Robertino, la vita è bella." (Life is beautiful.) One of her favorite phrases, which she sang in Italian, sounded like Ka Ja Fa, (What should I do?). Her exuberant ignorance was from another era, but I missed her now that she was only a phantom from my past.

I now walked past a plastered wall where there had once been a small room, the room where my friend Pasquale used to sit. From this small portal he had watched the people entering and leaving the courtyard, a student of their habits and manners. And I was the beneficiary of his informed gossip. "Signora Giuseppina came home early from work today in a foul mood," he would tell me. "Dom Carlo must be upset with his wife. He ran out of the courtyard in a huff again." "Luigi has pulled off one of his good deals, Roberto; you could see the smugness plastered on his face." "And the idiot Franco is in from Rome to visit his aunt. He thinks he's a big man because he's from the capital city. Little does he know that no one gives a shit about that kind of thing."

I thought about how as a child I had taken in these bits of wisdom with seriousness, how I was amazed at Pasquale's powers of observation, and how he had confided in me, a mere child. His wisdom was dispensed deliberately in small and steady morsels with immaculate timing and with stoic resolve. So his words always impressed me as grave and resolute.

Pasquale's wife, Titina, was corpulent and bawdy, sporting a meaty pimple in the middle of her face. Her philosophy of life did not have the nuances of Pasquale's observations. It was distilled into a few exacting words. As she worked in the garden wielding shovels, pails, and rakes, she would call out, "Robertino, Robertino." I took this to mean, "This is life. It's the same thing every day."

A few years after my yearly trips ended, I heard that Pasquale had died. The matter-of-fact way I heard about his passing, as if it were as expected and natural as winter turning into spring, only made the pain stronger. "Robertino, Robertino" I imagined Titina saying. Now the plaster wall covering the room where he had lived, observed, and absorbed so much of life seemed only to erase his memory, as if he had never existed.

I then remembered how, sometimes in the courtyard at night, Mrs. Malvese, whose house (actually a small room) faced Pasquale's, was outside feeding her granddaughter. The little girl was apparently uncooperative and refused to eat sometimes, for "Cacciavite" (the woman who catches lives), as she called herself, was focusing her attention on all the "bad" children.

This scene obviously made an impact on more than her granddaughter. My aunt's house was on the second story above the courtyard, and a translucent wall of glass enclosed one of her rooms. My aunt's maid would sometimes turn on a light behind herself and project her own shadow against the glass, making it visible in the courtyard. She would then take a broom and "ride" it as she ran back and forth between the light and the window. To add to the illusion, her nose was large and crooked, so her image cast against the glass made for a horrifying, much larger than life apparition. She would scream and yell in a high-pitched voice, "This is Cacciavite, the bad witch. Eat your food or I'm going to get you." The poor child downstairs was so frightened that she would shake like a leaf in a storm and gulp down her food to keep the witch away.

The glass was now painted white, and the "wicked witch" had been dead for thirty years.

Now I left the courtyard and walked into the street leading to the hub of the city. Gone was Giuseppino, sitting in his wicker chair, straw hat in hand, examining each passerby as if observing a thief. He would always signal me to come over so he could tease me about almost anything. I remember his asking once why we didn't have cheese in America. When I insisted that we did, he looked deliberately skeptical, as if to tell me, "I am letting you go because you are just a boy, but I have serious doubts about the cheese."

Gone also was Donna Carolina, the small, stooped woman dressed in black who appeared to be 100 years old and was no more than 4 1/2 feet tall. Her "shop" was an enclave carved out of the stone wall of a building. I remembered how she pulled all of her magical wares from the small grotto carved out behind her.

Now gone were the cacophonous noises of vendors screaming out about their wares and the music of women on terraces yelling to each other across the streets. Gone my immersion in the life of the street. Now I walked through it, a sole surveyor of its ghostly memories.

When I came to the open, nearly desolate Piazza Plebiscito, with a blazing sun on my face, I thought of that story my mother had told me: that in 1938 she had seen Mussolini and Hitler in this piazza and had not joined in on the wild enthusiasm of the crowd. A Carabiniere had seen the fear in her eyes and had nodded in approval.

At that time it might have been an omen of dark times, but for me now it brought back a simple question: Why had I been so attached to Naples in a way that could not be explained merely by the life of my Italian family, by the youthful joys of summer, and by the vivid encounters of its people?

On this 2004 trip I visited many other parts of the city with my wife and children. Unlike them, I was more than a tourist exploring unfamiliar sights. I was mining a dark, unknown terrain that had become an important part of who I was. When it was time to leave for the airport for our trip back home, my daughter cried; not wanting to make it worse for her, I betrayed no emotion, as if to reinforce that I was leaving a place of little importance.

I thought of my parents, now living in the Bronx in their later years, American, but only to some extent. They comment on America's politics, on its achievements, and on some of the "newer" aspects of popular culture. VCRs, IPods, tattoos, and cable television with "too many channels" are enigmas, modern fads that they look on with bewilderment and amusement. In Naples, when they had been married, they had just emerged from a war that started when they were not much older than my daughter was now. Naples was the intersection of their lives, where the recent past, both tragic and triumphant, met a new future in a new world. I thought about how this past pulled at me with its long tentacles.

On the way home I also thought of Pasquale, Maria, my family, Ischia and its beauties and secrets, and the past, fathomless and now—except for those tiny pieces of it still attached to me—dissolved into nothingness. Over many years, like eyes that eventually adjust to see objects in the dark, the pieces of history I had absorbed enveloped Naples like a clear light that settled into the corners of its winding streets. Like building blocks mounted slowly and carefully to construct a steady house, stories of family and Holocaust would become a bricked, impenetrable edifice within me. And so these stories of Naples still remain and keep defining me in ways that I cannot begin to understand.